M000033484

A Crisis in Culture

Fr. George William Rutler

A Crisis in Culture
How Secularism Is
Becoming a Religion

Edited by Mary Claire Kendall

EWTN PUBLISHING, INC.
Irondale, Alabama

EWTN Publishing, Inc.
5817 Old Leeds Road, Irondale, AL 35210

Distributed by Sophia Institute Press, Box 5284, Manchester, NH 03108.

paperback ISBN 978-1-68278-115-9

ebook ISBN 978-1-68278-116-6

Library of Congress Control Number: 2020944630

First printing

To the patient people of my parish

Contents

A Crisis in Culture

For the reader, the author notes that these chapters are transcripts of television talks and thus are in a style more conversational than formal prose.

The University's Identity Crisis

Universities are having their own crisis in our culture today. It is an identity crisis of cataclysmic proportions that has impacted Catholic universities just as severely but with even greater consequences.

Consider a line from an historic Church document. Bishops, it says, should show brotherly care for their fellow bishops who are harassed by calumny and other hardships for their Christian faith—and who may even suffer imprisonment or otherwise be impeded in the exercise of their ministry. It sounds like a line from the Council of Nicaea in A.D. 325, when so many bishops arrived bearing wounds from imperial Roman persecutions. Of course, any era of the Church could have produced such a line. But it is notable that, in fact, it comes from the Second Vatican Council's Decree of the Pastoral Office of Bishops, *Christus Dominus*, concerning the life of bishops. Not surprising, considering that the twentieth century saw more suffering for the faith than all Christian centuries combined—with more bishops martyred for their faith through the shedding of blood. It has persisted and is ongoing as I write, though it may receive limited coverage in the newspapers. "Wet martyrdom" through the shedding of blood is, of course, the kind of faith witness we are most familiar with.

A Crisis in Culture

There is also what we call "dry martyrdom," which is an interior suffering, a persecution by word, by slander, by opprobrium, by social rejection. It is this kind of suffering to which bishops are conspicuously exposed in our culture — on university campuses. I am not exaggerating. The attitudes that underlie it are so bad that one distinguished bishop said at the close of the twentieth century that he would rather send young people to some secular university where they would have to defend their faith than to some so-called Catholic university where they could have their faith taken away. An astounding statement but grounded in experience.

What is at work here? As the university asks, "What is a university; what is it supposed to be doing," the Catholic school, the Catholic university, goes a step further. It asks not only what it means to be a university but what it means to be a Catholic university. We have not done a very good job of living out the answer, which is a strange paradox considering that Catholicism gave the world the university.

The recognizable university came into being in the thirteenth century — in Paris, Oxford, and Bologna. But even then, certain tensions existed in the intellectual community between the revealed truth of Christ as the central governing locus for all fields of scientific endeavor and individual attempts to define and regulate the central truth of life. The emperor Fredrick II established a university in Naples in that century, and he tried to minimalize the clerical presence because he, as emperor, wanted to be the chief authority and chancellor — that is to say, ultimately, the definer of Truth with a capital "T." In Chartres, home of the majestic cathedral, a professor, with a master of arts in theology, no less, tried to establish a kind of rival to the Easter celebrations in the form of a pseudo-nature mysticism. (Nothing new here. That kind of pseudo-piety mixed with rationalism is encountered every day on our campuses.) Things got so bad that at the University of Paris, in the thirteenth century, the number of masters of theology had to be reduced to about half a dozen in order to introduce a semblance of quality control.

John Henry Newman was one of the great university figures of all time — an intellectual, a philosopher of education, the founder of a university. When he wrote about a university, he said that when a Catholic university does not practice its faith, this is hypocrisy. Take careful note that he does not say it is a mere mistake. Nor does he say it is inadequate. He says it is hypocrisy, plain and simple. That is because Catholicism is the essence — the very heart — of the identity of the Catholic university. Just as Catholicism gave us the university, so is a Catholic university the fulfillment of the unifying tradition of the arts, to which all intellectual enterprise of whatever kind tends. And when a Catholic university claims to be Catholic in ethos, in cultural tradition, in spirit, in custom, but not in what it teaches and in how it lives, hypocritical is the only way to characterize the situation. Such a university is not revealing its true self. It is wearing a mask, if you will — and not to stay free of some pandemic but to keep from living out its true identity, the source of its very existence, as a Catholic university.

The seedlings of the university were planted in the fifth century in Byzantium — Constantinople, to be exact — in the imperial court schools. They were more of a Christianized version of the old court training school for diplomats. This rough approximation of a university was founded by a woman, Aelia Eudocia Augusta, also known as "Saint Eudocia," who was the wife of the emperor Theodosius II. Its purpose was to provide a court of educated aides to serve the imperial government. (Interestingly, in Western culture since the Second World War, diplomacy and foreign affairs have become a recognized academic discipline in our universities, repeating this old courtly tradition, for good or for ill.)

A Crisis in Culture

Even before Eudocia, in the fourth century, the old Greek academies were also being Christianized. Which is to say, the cult had been changed, for the academy was already centrally identified by the gods it worshipped. When Christianity was legalized, the pantheon, the hall, the shrine of the gods of the universities was Christianized, whereby worship of the gods was replaced with true worship focused on the one true God, Christ the Savior. But this was more of an architectural adjustment than a deep philosophical or spiritual change. In this regard, more than one theologian has pointed out that, in the Athenium, you had studying side by side the great St. Basil and Julian the Apostate, the emperor who would repudiate the legalization of Christianity. We may computerize offices, we may pasteurize milk, but we do not "Christianize" schools. Christianity is not a gloss we put on the curriculum; it is not an architectural statement we make by putting a chapel on the campus. It is not a public declaration we make by appointing a few theology professors to the faculty.

The Christian identity of a university is the presence of Christ as the focus of truth and the model of the spiritual and moral well-being of the institution. Underscoring this fact, the same foundress of the first university, Eudocia, wrote a story about a magician of Antioch named Cyprianus. (In fact, it was upon this story, probably, that the Faust legend was based.) Cyprianus sells his soul to the devil. He wants facts, and, in his haste, he sells his soul to the prince of lies. Oh, he gets lots of truths around him but at the expense of the living truth. Any university can do that. It is very easy to establish a department of a particular science here, and a department of a particular science there, researching, discovering details about the world, but while totally ignoring the Creator of the world. Such a university has lost a sense of the universe.

We might say that the first university was really in the Garden of Eden. The University of Eden was founded by Adam and

Eve. They wanted to redefine reality on their own terms, and they sold their souls to the prince of lies. In nineteenth-century New England, it was said that the best school was a log, with a student at one end and Mark Hopkins, president of Williams College, at the other. You see, Hopkins was something of a philosopher, but a distinguished educator. Well, whatever else that log was, it was not felled from the tree of the knowledge of good and evil. That tree in the Garden of Eden represented reality. If we knock that tree down, we do not have the truth. We may sit on it. We may claim that we are the masters of truth, but all we have are little facts, and we have very little in the way of education.

What was the motive behind the foundation of the University of Eden? Our friend John Henry Newman gives the answer. He says, "Quarry the granite rock with razors or moor the vessel with a thread of silk and then you may hope with such keen and delicate instruments of human knowledge and human wisdom to contend against those giants—the *passion and pride of man.*"[1] I think that's one of the finest lines ever uttered: "the passion and pride of man." And it is as easy to conquer them as it is to quarry a rock with a razor, or to moor a vessel with a thread of silk. That is to say, it's nearly impossible!

The crisis of our universities today shows the potency of passion and pride. Passion refined by a university becomes zeal for the truth, but if it is passion on only the natural level, then it succumbs to what Cardinal Newman warned would be pluralism—the surrender of truth for the sake of compromise, popular approval, economic gain, government charters and funding. Pride, refined in the university, becomes courage for the truth, but Newman warned that selfish pride in the university will water down Catholic truth so

---

[1] John Henry Newman, *The Idea of a University* 1, 5, 9.

that, in the name of broad-mindedness, it becomes half-truth, and half-truth is always a lie.

It has often been said that when the Church is in a corrupt society, She will be attacked from without. When She is corrupt Herself, She will be attacked from within. The same is true of so-called Catholic universities. When they are faithful to the faith, they will be attacked from society, from outside. When they are corrupt within, they will become living contradictions of themselves.

St. Gregory of Nyssa told the story of an entertainer in the marketplace in Alexandria, a very little man lavishly dressed and very acrobatic. Crowds would gather around to see him do extraordinary somersaults and things. On one occasion, someone threw nuts on the ground, and the figure pulled off a mask: it was a monkey. The monkey scrambled for the nuts, and the people realized what they had been watching. There are a lot of universities that fit that description in our culture. They may, to all outward appearances, look elegant, graceful, well-costumed, and entertaining, but when they grasp for the things thrown to them, the mask comes off.

The Greeks knew that education—which they called *paideia*; the Latins called it *eruditus*, from which we derive the word *erudition*— had three functions. The first is teaching people how to live in a civilized society—basic social contracts that they enter into, certain disciplines that they study that make sense of what they are doing. The second function is moral formation, which is necessary lest our society fall apart. And the third is refinement of perception, so that people will be able to tell truths from falsehoods, beauty from ugliness, what works from what destroys.

It is interesting that in the entire classical tradition, the Greeks and the Latins liked to walk when they taught. The Greeks had a walking school. It was called the Peripatetic Academy. Socrates walked about ten miles a day as he taught. Aristotle gained major insight on a twenty-mile hike he took to Megara. From Christian history, we know that St. Cyril left his teacher, Photius, in the Byzantine academy and walked all the way to Great Moravia, establishing what we now know as Slavonic culture. And throughout the history of Christian civilization, we have seen monks such as Friar Bacon walking through the academy—Albert the Great and Aquinas too.

All because at the beginning of salvation history, Christ our Teacher walked among us. And on Easter, He appeared on the road to Emmaus between two men who were so engrossed in their lecturing back and forth that they did not at first discern Him. And He said to them, "How is it that you did not understand all that the prophets had spoken?" (see Luke 24:25). That is the voice of Christ to culture, and He speaks it through the university. He speaks it officially through His teachers, the bishops, who have the primary function of seeing to it that the universities proclaim that ultimate truth. Christ walks among us, and He sends his Apostles to remind us of His truth.

Pope St. John Paul II, on an apostolic journey to the United States, spoke about Catholic universities and pointed out that we have some 235 colleges and universities that call themselves Catholic, and they have done splendid things and have been some of the great jewels in the history of Catholicism. But he also sounded very much, I think, like St. Paul writing in his second letter to Timothy. "Preach the word," St. Paul said, "be urgent in season and out of season, convince, rebuke, and exhort, be unfailing in patience and in teaching. For the time is coming when people will not endure sound teaching, but having itching ears they will accumulate for themselves teachers to suit their own likings, and will turn away from listening to the truth and wander into myths" (2 Tim. 4:2-4). This has been the crisis of the Catholic university.

A convention of presidents of Catholic colleges and universities was held in 1967. In the most tragic and misguided way, they said that the Catholic university must assert its autonomy against every outside force, including that of Church authorities. But Church authorities are authorities only because Christ is the Author of Truth. To be autonomous that way is what the Greeks called idiocy. An idiot is one's own person—not just someone who thinks for himself but a person who thinks he is the *only* person. And that autonomous idiocy has been the plague of Catholic education in this past generation—living evidence of what Newman called "those giants, the passion and pride of man."

About a thousand years ago, there was what some called a dark age. It was not as dark as many think it was. It was conspicuous, however, for widespread ignorance. There were learned people, and there was learning. But there were no universities. Learning took refuge in the monasteries.

Today we have another dark age. It is not an age of ignorance. We have more information at our fingertips than any culture has ever known. This is a dark age of cynicism. In the first dark age, there was learning without universities. In our dark age, there are universities without learning. The university will recover its mission when it understands why it was sent into the world. That can be understood only by learning more and more how it is to be Catholic. It is the Catholic university that will remind other universities how they came into being and what their walk through culture portends. That means that the Catholic institutions have to remember once again that in their walk along the Emmaus road, they are doing a lot of talking, and they are talking so intently that they forget the one in their midst—the Teacher of nations, the only Teacher. And when He rose from the dead, Mary Magdalene called out to Him, "Rabbi, Teacher." He replied, "Do not cling to me" (John 20:16–17). "Do not hold on to my form. Do not hold on to my buildings. Do not cling to my outward signs." Universities have buildings, they have campuses, they have bell towers, but the truth is a living thing—Christ Himself! And that truth is mocked by buildings that forget what they were built for.

Veritas vos liberabit—"The truth shall set you free"! The truth is not to be clung to. It is to give life to culture, and it gives life to culture in one way: through the university. And the university will be free to be itself only when it understands that Christ is the Truth!

Cultural Healing through Truth

All sciences have their own vocabulary, and it's usually a very difficult vocabulary that only the inner circle can use. Bear in mind: the act of thinking is itself a science — a very refined science called philosophy. Its practitioners, philosophers, make their living discussing how we think. As for the mechanics of thinking, if you will, we leave that to the epistemologists who delve into the nuances of epistemology. Then there are the medical doctors, who must use clinical words. They have a lot of complex things to talk about relating to the health of the body, or the lack thereof. The body is a marvelous instrument, the greatest machine in the world.

St. Paul was a physician. Not a physician of the body, mind you. Although sometimes, like most people in those days, he did volunteer medical advice. Remember, he told Timothy he should try a little wine for his digestion (1 Tim. 5:23). But St. Paul was a physician of the mind. He writes in his First Letter to Timothy about people who are engaged in telling lies. In the sixth chapter he says, and I am paraphrasing, "Consider the people who deny the doctrines of Christ as we have received it, who substitute falsehoods for true religion. Such people must be recognized for their ignorance, their conceit, and they are sick in their love of controversy and polemics." Sick! He did not say *wrong* but *sick*!

A Crisis in Culture

Truth is not part of our outer skin — the thing that dermatologists concern themselves with. Rather, truth is the reality of our whole being, our very essence. God is our Creator, and He is Truth. If we tell lies, sickness sets into this life rooted in the divine Truth. And if we consecrate ourselves to lies, our sickness can be unto death. St. Paul was a physician of the mind, and he knew how the mind works and what happens when the mind works the wrong way. We are sick if we live lies. We instinctively know that. That is why we say, "That joke is sick," or "That film was sick." We don't simply say it was in bad taste or that it was erroneous. We know that it violates the dignity of man in one way or another. There is something in our nature that tells us naturally what we are, and when we see something at variance with our healthful state, we say it is sick.

There is a sickness in the way we think today. Quite simply, we are concerned not about how to think but about what to think: what we call "political correctness." And we store great amounts of information without having a clue as to how to think about it. In this regard, we love computers! Computers are a great invention. And we love what computers can tell us; and we love what we can tell computers. We can garner vast storehouses of information. We have made trivia into a science of its own. But the more we look at the screen and the more we see things, the more we can delude ourselves into thinking that we are thinking. In reality, we are only registering. If we do not know how to analyze, how to evaluate, how to judge, how mentally to discern truth from lies, we are not thinking. And we end up clueless about the *how* of the mind and know only the *what* of the mind. By that process, we are not rational. We only rationalize.

When we are armed with reams of facts, it is very easy to rationalize. In fact, the more facts we have, the more we can avoid true reason. Stalin, one of the most diabolical henchmen who ever lived, allegedly said, as quoted by newspaper columnist Leonard Lyons in 1947, "A single death is a tragedy; a million deaths is a statistic." That is the voice not only of a liar, but of the prince of lies, who brought the worst sickness of all into the world—death! I have stood at the grave of Stalin. It was one of the very few times in my life that I can say I smelled evil. Oh, the body was beyond corruption, buried underground. No, that was not the smell. But evil has a smell. It is the smell of a decay that rots culture after culture, that fragments civilizations, that decomposes families. It is the malignancy that eats away at the human soul. The Soviets used to tell their children in the state schools that there was no God and all the customs of the Church were superstition. They used to put holy water under a microscope to show the children that it looked no different from any other kind of water. That is the sickness of the mind that knows *what* to think but not *how* to think. Kill one man, it is murder; fifty thousand—a million—it is a strategy.

"How could any society have countenanced such a lie?" we ask. We do not have to look so far as Russia to ponder that question. We can look right in our own backyard and wonder why, if only one child in the United States in the last thirty years had been killed in his mother's womb, it would have been called "the social crime of the age." The media spotlight's intense glare would have focused on it as all the judges and legal experts discussed the grave consequences of so heinous a crime, and all the philosophers and sociologists debated how anyone could have been moved to do such a thing. Yet, now that it happens fifteen hundred times a day—ten, twenty, thirty million times in a generation, in one nation—it is called a political movement. That is a sickness! St. Paul recognized this way of thinking as a sickness. But, the dreadful sign of this sickness is that you do not know when you have it and are therefore incapable of curing yourself. The cure has to come

A Crisis in Culture

from outside. Our Lord says, "You have not chosen me: but I have chosen you" (John 15:16).

We do not make up the truth. The truth is given to us. The world was here before we were. We come into this world, and then, step by step, we become cognizant of the world around us. As St. Thomas Aquinas said, "Man has to be led to virtue gradually."[2] We do not see the whole picture at once. When we do, it is too frightening, and we shrink from it, and then, step by step, we try to approach it. That is why a baby cries when he is born into this larger world. The process of educating the human person in how to think means quite literally to lead him forth into reality—*educare*.

The Greeks, and Socrates in particular, spoke of the maieutic method of teaching, which derives from *maieutikos*, the Greek word for *midwifery*. In one of Plato's Dialogues, Socrates, whose mother was a midwife, used this method to bring forth new ideas through reasoning and dialogue, as analogous to the way a midwife brings forth and delivers a baby from the mother's womb. The teacher was the one who brought the unborn intellect into full social participation. For the Greeks, learning was really a matter of remembering what had essentially been sealed in our mind at our creation—which, as we grow older, we recover and analyze logically.

The Church, the paramount teacher of nations, is called "Holy Mother." Even our schools are called *alma mater*, our "beloved mother," that eternal figure who brings the youngest in the culture into the presence of the oldest wisdom. The Church is not a building; the Church is not a chancellery; the Church is the Mother who leads us to the truth of the Son. Fittingly enough, Our Lady is called the Seat of Wisdom, *Sedes Sapentia*. The founder of the Catholic education system in this country is St. Elizabeth Ann Seton, whom

[2] See St. Thomas Aquinas, *Summa Theologica* I-II, q. 96, art. 2.

16

we instinctively call "Mother." The same holds true for Mother Cabrini, whose formal name—St. Frances Cabrini—also recognizes her canonization. The sanctity of both these women—these mothers—consisted of maternal educating of a culture. A mother knows that the young have souls. And Holy Mother Church knows the contents of the soul; this is why the Church is best equipped in culture to teach us not only what to think but how to think. Instinctively, if someone rebels against the truth, it is because he thinks it is restrictive. "Who are you to teach me how to think?" The Church answers, "Your Mother, the Mother of all culture, the Mother who leads you to the truth." Our Mother knows what a soul is. Our Mother knows that the soul has an intellect, the soul has a will, and the soul also has an imagination. The Church has guided the intellectual part of the soul in the form of the new *Catechism* (1992). She has helped form the will through the *Code of Canon Law* (1983). And She has guided our imagination through Her encyclical letters, which reveal that there is a truth and how we are to perceive that truth.

I suppose, in a special way, the encyclical *Veritatis Splendor* opens the imagination to the glory of the truth— not just the evidence of facts, the indisputability of little truths, but the *Splendor of the Truth* itself.

In the late sixteenth century, there was a saintly Jesuit named Peter Canisius, who, for a year or so, was appointed administrator of the Diocese of Vienna in Austria. It is sobering to reflect that, when he went to Vienna, that city, the seat of the old Holy Roman Empire, had not had one single ordination to the priesthood for nineteen long years. Such was the condition of the Church at the time. And how do you suppose he responded? Of course, he got right to work to rectify the situation. Among his many reforms, he published a catechism that was so popular it was translated into nine languages and went through fifty-five editions — a remarkable record for any time, and especially for some four hundred years ago!

Our Church did much the same thing again through the publication of the *Catechism of the Catholic Church* some thirty years ago. The fruits have been considerable — not just by telling us what to think, but by putting before us the whole splendor of the truth to which we are called through obedience. In 1983, in a French journal, *L'Homme Nouveau* (The new man), a writer stated that by the end of the twentieth century, history books will recall that the most important event in the Church's understanding of how to learn the truth took place in conferences at the Cathedral of Notre Dame that Cardinal Joseph Ratzinger, the future Pope Benedict XVI, convened. In this series of conferences, the then prefect of the Congregation for the Doctrine of the Faith in Rome lamented that, for years, people had come to think that we do not need a catechism; that we do not need to address the sickness that has afflicted the way we think. I am not exaggerating when I speak of the sickness. Deconstruction is a sick thing in architecture. It is destructive. It is a sicker thing in the mind. Yet it has become a whole school — not of thinking but of unthinking. Literature is analyzed, not according to what the author meant but according to what we want the author to have meant. To some, this applies not only to Shakespeare but also to the Bible and to the God of the Bible. This goes only so far. The most distinguished actors, including the likes of Ethel Barrymore and her siblings John and Lionel, considered it their highest duty to convey what the playwright intended.

Our Holy Mother, the Church, has worked assiduously to bring our culture to rebirth — essentially functioning as the midwife of a culture in crisis. It is a high calling in this age, when culture is crumbling all around us — statues of revered figures being torn down in 2020 at a frightening pace. Part of this crisis consists of our inability to locate the authority behind truth—the voice that tells us that there is a truth and where the truths behind or within this ultimate truth are to be located. Our society is suspicious of authorities. Our society uses the term *authority* almost as a pejorative because many authorities have disappointed them. Rather than reforming, where needed, too often we see a breakdown in the proper exercise of authority—a breakdown that is sometimes the result of pride. It takes humility for a legitimate authority to exercise the proper office, to use discipline, to say that right is right, and wrong is wrong, to impose penalties. It is so much easier to be popular, to be Mr. Nice Guy. But a true authority recognizes that there is a truth to which that authority itself is accountable. And yet, more and more, authorities subordinate their opinion to the opinions of celebrities. Consider how many committees in Congress hold on to celebrities' every word—not because celebrities speak with authority but because the masses put them on a pedestal of popularity. The Kardashians, famous for being famous, are a prime example. Then, too, I like to think back to the late eighties, when three Hollywood actresses testified before a committee on agriculture. Why? Simply because they had played the parts of farmers' wives in some popular films. One celebrity, who at the time I knew only as Whoopi Something-or-other, testified in Washington on the national debt, not knowing anything at all about the subject, but testifying on the basis of her celebrity.

This is the sickness that comes into a deconstructive culture. If we do not look to Christ as the source of authority, we will try to invent a substitute, a synthetic truth. There is nothing wrong with synthetic fabrics, but a synthetic truth is a disease. Synthesis as the means to truth has been the philosopher's stone of many illusionists—in which regard, many of these philosophers have thought that truth itself is only a synthesis of ideas or forces. In the 2020s, we have reaped the whirlwind.

A Crisis in Culture

In Rome, there is a statue of a man named Giordano Bruno, who died in the year 1600. At least, I think it's still there, unless the rabble has torn that down as well. Though, unlikely, for Giordano Bruno is considered in many ways a hero of "free thought." He influenced the philosophy of Leibniz, among others, and was basically an atheist in outlook. Not so long ago, it was discovered that Bruno was most likely an anti-Catholic spy for the Elizabethan government of England, responsible for bringing many priests to death. He himself was burned at the stake in an unjustifiable way. Irrespective of the injustice by which he died, the fact is, what he taught was a lie that sickened much of culture.

Leibniz taught that "truth is the daughter of time." In other words, we find truth only through experimentation in the first place. A fair enough idea, but he taught that truth itself is always in flux; that there is no objective truth; that only our version of reality is what counts. Yes, we have reaped the whirlwind.

Of course, this whirlwind of sickness totally contradicts the voice that said, "I AM the Way, the Truth, and the Life" (see John 14:6). When Our Lord was asked how old He was, He said, "Before Abraham was, I AM" (John 8:58). He is the Lord of history, the God of time.

Truth, then, is not the daughter of time. Time is the daughter of truth. God is truth and He set time in motion, and that motion we call tradition. If we want to know how to think, we have to understand tradition—which literally means a "handing down" of the truth, God's truth. This is the only truth, and it is unchanging. We are living traditions of our elders. Their chromosomes flow through our bodies, and God's truth flows through history, in Sacred Tradition—not nostalgia, but the truths passed on from age to age by people who have taken the reality of truth seriously and have let it develop in their own cultural idiom. That is why Cardinal Newman spoke of the development of doctrine not as the invention of doctrine or replacement of previous doctrine, but in the way a photograph develops. Tradition is always there with certain discernible characteristics, he says. If we want to know how to think about tradition, there is a tradition of principle.

The truth is always there. There is an assimilation of the truth in every culture. There is a logical sequence to how that truth develops. There is a chronic vigor to it and a conservation of the old that always has integrity. If we do not have a tradition, we stop thinking. We have the Creed, we have the sacraments, we have the life of prayer, and we have the commandments — all as part of the tradition of thought. A young student said to the professor at the end of a lecture, "You speak about the Second World War. Isn't that the one that was in black and white?" That's all he knew about the war. If that's all we know about life, that it's black and white, our life will be gray. The truth brings beauty and color. And light.

Christianity and Common Sense

Thomas Paine was one of the prime propagandists of the American Revolution. His pamphlet *Common Sense*—an impassioned plea for American independence from Great Britain—was one of the best sellers of all time. Yet the irony is, he was conspicuously lacking in common sense himself. This curious deficit was on display when he went to France and became a propagandist for the political machine that ushered in the "Reign of Terror." He thought that common sense consisted of denying the truths of God. In spite of it all, he has become something of a folk hero for our country. Go to New Rochelle, New York, and visit his house there, preserved for posterity. There is no exhibit devoted to his disordered mind. Yet the fact is, he is the very embodiment of the malfunctioning of the human mind.

He is not alone. Many of those with exceedingly clever minds have lacked basic common sense. George Bernard Shaw, for one, used to mock Christianity allegedly for not being sensible. Given his erroneous perception, he became a propagandist in a more than subtle way for the communists as they began to terrorize the Russian people—to Lenin's undying gratitude. His "useful idiots," Lenin called Shaw and others like him. Yet the irony is, Christianity is, in fact, steeped in common sense. It reveals the right ordering of the mind, and the right ordering of the mind is the essence of common sense. St. Thomas Aquinas made some of the most perceptive contributions in this regard through treatises he wrote on how to explain the faith to those who find it difficult to accept or who reject it outright. In *Summa Contra Gentiles*, his treatise against the Gentiles, he said, "We have to use the mind in appealing to the minds of others." When we are dealing with Christian heretics, we can argue from the New Testament because they accept that. When we are arguing with Jews, we can argue from the Old Testament because they accept that. But when we argue with Muslims and others who accept neither the Old nor the New Testament, we must simply appeal to reason.

Reason is the weapon of the saints. The alternative to Christianity is not reason but superstition. Years ago, in my city of New York, during a mayoral campaign, a Hollywood celebrity endorsed one of the candidates. At a press conference, she was asked a very sensible question: "Why?" Why, indeed, was she supporting her chosen candidate? No one had bothered to ask her that question, and she amazed the audience by saying, "In a previous reincarnation, he and I were married."

That is what I mean by the superstition that corrupts the mind when it is not rightly ordered according to God's truth.

The apostate French bishop in the eighteenth to early-nineteenth century, Charles Maurice de Talleyrand-Périgord said of the French royal family — the Bourbons — that they remembered everything and learned nothing. They knew their history, they were proud of their lineage, they could diagram their family tree, they remembered all the offenses made against the family. But it was all somewhat beside the point because they had learned nothing from their own mistakes. And so, tragically, perhaps the most sincere, reforming moral of them, King Louis XVI, became the last of the line because, with all those interests and virtues, he conspicuously lacked common sense. The same might be said of that good man Nicholas II, the last czar of Russia, who died a noble death—perhaps we could say a holy death—a man dedicated to making some modest reforms in the economy and social structure of his land, a man totally dedicated to his family and yet a man lacking, in so many instances, in basic common sense. So much so, that records unsealed in 2017 revealed that not even his cousin King George V, who was his spitting image and played with him as a child, would grant him and his family asylum in Great Britain lest the Windsors, themselves steeped in common sense, more often than not, go down like the Romanovs.

Christianity constantly enlivens the mind. Catholic universities exist as witness to that truth. When we are left with only the mind without the structure by which it is rightly ordered, however, then common sense becomes the victim. That is why common sense is so conspicuously absent in so many of our centers of learning. To illustrate this phenomenon, consider the drama that unfolded after a Catholic university in the United States decided, in 1992, to give an honorary degree to Joseph Cardinal Ratzinger, the future Pope Benedict XVI, then prefect of the Congregation for the Doctrine of the Faith. He is a man who vividly witnesses to the neutral employment of the life of the mind and the life of the heart, a man of intellectual integrity and true piety. Act I: The faculty of Science did not object to this honor. Act II: The faculty of Law did not. Act III: Some voices in the faculty of Theology vigorously objected. They said he was too controversial. Truth will always be controversial in an age of lies. And, so, the honor was not conferred. Act IV: Shortly thereafter, the Académie des Sciences Morales et Politiques (Academy of Moral and Political Sciences) elected that same Cardinal Ratzinger to fill the vacancy left by Andrey Sakharov. Sakharov was, of course, the distinguished Russian Jew, scientist, Nobel laureate and civil rights advocate who helped bring about the downfall of the Marxist tyranny in his own country.

A Crisis in Culture

What a vivid commentary on how, as Our Lord reminded us, the people of this world sometimes are cleverer than the children of light! The French Academy is not a Catholic institution, but it recognizes the integrity of the intellect, rightly employed. In his inaugural address, Cardinal Ratzinger said, speaking as a German who knew the penalties of living with Nazis and living with communists, "There was never a single action which was regarded as evil in itself." Speaking of the Nazi regime in particular, he said, "Over whole decades, a collapse of the moral sense was taking place. It was bound to be transformed into total nihilism on the day when any of the preceding goals no longer had any value, and when freedom was synonymous with the ability to do whatever was capable of providing a passing attraction and interest to a life which had become empty."[3]

A life that had become empty: Frei aber einsam ("Free but lonely") as the saying goes. When we lack common sense to recognize objective truth, the entire moral order of society collapses. We are no longer guided by truth. The mind cannot be rightly ordered. It seeks only distraction and pleasure. And when those twin empty diversions fail to satisfy, the mind moves on to another distraction, another pleasure, and so becomes addicted to frenzy and to lies. That, you see, is the decay of the mind.

There are those who look upon the culture crisis in which we live and say, as in the cynical political campaign slogan "It's the economy, stupid." That's what matters. Judas Iscariot was saying essentially the same thing. After all, he criticized the woman for wasting money by pouring precious ointment on Our Lord. But Our Lord reminded Judas, and He reminds all of us: it's not the

---

[3] Joseph Cardinal Ratzinger, "On Sakharov and Rorty: Without Morality, Liberty Is Impossible," *Crisis Magazine*, May 1, 1993, https://www.crisismagazine.com/1993/on-sakharov-and-rorty-without-morality-liberty-is-impossible.

economy, stupid, that is at the heart of our culture crisis. It is the decomposition of the soul. It is the wrong ordering of the intellect away from the heart.

The crisis in society is the crisis in our perception of good and evil. Cardinal Ratzinger reminds us that every tyranny denies the objectivity of the moral order. This is why we have moved into a new kind of sickness in moral perception. No longer are we confronted with immorality so much as with amorality. It is like what that comedian said about public figures: that now they lie but they don't twitch. That is not immorality; it is amorality, and it is born of that nonsensical denial of the objectivity of the moral order.

The resolution of this amorality is not going to come through some kind of facile reaction, as we see in the people who speak rather glibly in political terms. A case in point is neoconservatism, which was touted as an anecdote for the problem. Neoconservatism was the policies of those liberals who described themselves as "mugged by reality." But if a liberal is mugged, all we have is a neoconservative. He is not a saint. He is not a guardian of authentic moral culture. To be a saint, we have to be mugged by reality. Neoconservatism, whose power has waned, is not adequate. Nor is neoliberalism, perhaps back on the ascent, the answer. As St. Josemaría Escrivá de Balaguer wrote, "These world crises are crises of saints."[4]

Just so. The resolution of our culture crisis consists in confronting the truth of Christ. This is precisely what St. Paul did after initially engaging in hounding Christians before his conversion. He was on the Road to Damascus to hound more. Then he heard a voice that essentially said, "Saul, Saul, why are you mugging Me?" Saul realized that Christ was in each one of those people he was offending and hurting by his mugging and that Christ was in

---

[4] Josemaría Escrivá, *The Way*, no. 301.

the culture that he was destroying. And in that moment, Saul the mugger became Paul the mugged. His life was changed—assaulted by reality. For this reason, Christianity teaches what we call a realist metaphysics—a big term for the Church's commitment to the way things really are. The world has been assaulted by reality in the most splendid way, when "the Word became flesh and dwelt among us" (John 1:14).

Realist metaphysics means not believing something because we think it but thinking something because it exists. "That is in the mind which is first in the senses" is the old Scholastic principle that goes back before the Christian revelation to some of the perceptions of the Greek philosophers. They perceived the truth, using copious common sense, in two ways: the purity of truth and the order of truth. This is a kind of *Reader's Digest* version of philosophical history, but suffice it to say that Plato emphasized the purity of truth, and drawing on him, so did St. Augustine. Aristotle, on the other hand, emphasized the order of truth, and drawing on him, so did St. Thomas Aquinas. Both traditions are noble, and they cannot be glibly separated one from the other because they draw on one another and respect one another. But both can also be corrupted.

The emphasis on the purity of the truth is corrupted by what we call dualism. The dualists disdain common sense. They see that there is a spiritual order, they see there is a natural order, but they ignore the logic by which the same Creator Who is in heaven made this world. The dualist separates the two. That is how we got that perennial heresy called Gnosticism, which is like a simmering pot all through the history of human perception—asserting that there is a spiritual world up there and the terrestrial world here, and the two are at enmity.

Less than a thousand years ago, Gnosticism was a resurrected problem in Christianity in the form of the Albigensian heretics. St. Dominic fought against them. The chivalric St. Louis IX, king of France, fought against them. And Simon de Montfort led his troops against them. We may wonder why the Albigensians were so harshly dealt with. The reason is quite simple. If they had prevailed, they would have destroyed Western civilization due to their lack of common sense. Their dualism denied the integrity of marriage. It denied the integrity of sexual morality. The Albigensians went so far as to promote suicide as the ultimate solution for society's ills — the ultimate symptom of a lack of common sense.

Even though it was destroyed a millennium ago, this kind of fantasy keeps cropping up in our day. Remember the song called "Imagine" by the Beatles' John Lennon? It describes the way the world should be according to his likes, and it is gratuitously sentimental, for it speaks of a world without hatred, without war, but also ultimately a world without religion and religion's God. It is through this dualism that we get fantasies such as Christian Science, New Age religiosity, deconstruction in literary analysis; and in the political order, most vividly Marxism, which is a form of Gnosticism — a dream of building a Utopia that would confound both heaven and earth and thereby redefine reality. The Marxists were politically correct. They revised history if it did not satisfy them. They exploited the intelligentsia and the media. They had an intellectual elite, which set the tone for the perception of reality, all in obedience to what they considered the purity of truth. But this obedience was a nonsensical distortion of truth's purity.

In the same way, the emphasis on the order of truth was distorted through what we call naturalism, which is the polar opposite of dualism. Naturalism does not deny the good of creation. It says that creation itself is divine. That is how we got pantheism, how we got transcendentalist philosophy in our country in the nineteenth century and those utopian communities of Ralph Waldo Emerson and the like. It is how we got radical feminism and social Darwinism. And just as dualism ended up politically as Marxism, so in our time did naturalism end up as fascism, Nazism, and now anarchist movements that seek to destroy political free speech in our country and demand obedience to the anarchists' tenets. The great goal, then as now, was not paradise, paradise on earth, as Marxism claimed; it was power. And the champion was not the common man, the masses; it was the superman.

If we are dualists, we will lose the season of Advent, which reminds us of the consanguinity, if you will — the harmony — of heaven with earth through contemplating the four great truths of death, judgment, heaven, and hell. If we do not want to use enough common sense to admit their reality, we will deny the season of Advent and pretend that all year is Christmas, and, by so doing, we will lose both Advent and Christmas. And, if we are naturalists, we will lose a sacrament — the sacrament of Confession — for we will not want to look into the heart of fallen nature.

Christianity is the greatest bequeathal of common sense to the world, for Christianity tells us that if we want to perceive reality, we will not perceive it through the imaginings of our own minds. We will sense it through the experience of the Church through history — *sentire cum ecclesia*: to know things by sensing them with our Holy Mother, the Church. Reality is real. Reality speaks to us through human experience. Our mind is given to us by God to analyze that. But to undertake that analysis, we must have humility, which is the ground of common sense.

Pope St. John Paul II, reflecting in those interviews with Italian journalist Vittorio Messori published in *Crossing the Threshold of Hope*, looks back upon the day when he was shot. "Perhaps this is why it was necessary for the assassination attempt to be made in St. Peter's Square precisely on May 13, 1981, the anniversary of the first apparition at Fatima," he said, "so that all could become more transparent and comprehensible, so that the voice of God which speaks in human history through the 'signs of the times' could be more easily heard and understood."[5] The pope was reminding us that God does indeed speak through the "signs of the times," but we can miss them if we do not use our minds the right way.

When Our Lord walked on the road to Emmaus, He asked those two men, "How can you be so slow of heart to believe all that was spoken of by the prophets?" In other words, "Why are you so deficient in perception?" The astonishing fact is that exactly what He was referencing had happened: He was raised from the dead. To those literal-minded people who define reality according to their small perception, that is the most senseless thing we could ever claim—that a man should die and rise again. And yet it happened, and we know it happened because it was real in time and space. It was sensed, and for that reason, it impinged upon the mind. St. John said essentially, "Our eyes saw it, our hands handled it" (see 1 John 1:1). When Our Lord appeared in the Upper Room to His Apostles, He said to Thomas, "Put your finger here, and see my hands; and put out your hand, and place it in my side; do not be faithless, but believing" (John 20:27). He took a honeycomb and a fish and ate them. He said, "A spirit has not flesh and bones as you see that I have" (Luke 24:39, 42–43, Douay-Rheims). This is the perennial appeal of Christ to common sense. All through history, He makes those appeals.

And He is making it now to you and to me. It is Christ in His Church Who shows the right ordering of the mind. The strange thing about common sense is that it is really not that common at all. Indeed, the great gospel that we proclaim to the nations is that, as far as common sense goes, "Jesus Christ is the only One Who ever really had it."

---

[5] His Holiness John Paul II, *Crossing the Threshold of Hope* (New York: Alfred A. Knopf, 1995), 131–132.

The Prayer of the Church

Letter writing is becoming a lost art because of the digital revolution. As a result, historians in centuries to come are going to find it difficult to write about our age and those who shaped it. By looking at letters of various figures presented in history books—not only the famous but, perhaps more revealing, those who have made less of a mark—we discern a common tradition of the human personality. And that is that the same concerns occupy people of all generations. All those little details that historians do not think are very important until four hundred or five hundred years later are recorded in the intimate correspondence of people who had no earthly idea that their letters would ever be saved. They were just living their lives.

Then, too, letter writing develops one's literary ability. That is why, in France, Mademoiselle Jeanne Françoise Julie Adélaïde Récamier apologized to a friend for writing so long a letter. She said, "I didn't have enough time to write a shorter one"—the hallmark of good literature, of course, being an economy of words. Apropos of which, in the New Testament, the more the letter writers speak of a love of God, the shorter their letters become, the more intense, the more skilled, because the Holy Spirit is ever more vividly the writer.

A Crisis in Culture

Prayer is correspondence between man and God, and we will always need to correspond with our Creator. And just as letter writing is replaced by e-mail and other things, so God will correspond with us in one way or another, but it will always be prayer. Of course, it is possible for people to fantasize sometimes and to mistake the correspondent for God when, in truth, it is only their ego. Someone once said that when people talk to God, it's prayer; when God talks to them, it's schizophrenia. Mind you, there are a great many schizophrenics in the religious realm, such as that woman who told the preacher that as she crossed Broadway she got a message from Our Lady to tell him he should convert Hitler. To this the preacher kindly and sagely responded, "Well, I just received a message too, and Our Lady told me to forget that."

The more a society is in crisis, and the more confusion there is within the Church, the more people will easily seek signs and wonders and fantasize about apparitions and locutions. It can be schizophrenia. It can be private schizophrenia, it can be a social schizophrenia, but this does not denigrate the integrity of authentic prayer. God corresponds with us and we with Him. I once sat at a kitchen table with St. Teresa of Calcutta and asked her how really to preach. And she said, "Make your meditation and then go in and tell the people what Jesus told you." That is the voice of someone in close correspondence with God. It is prayer, which is the intimate conversation of the human heart with the Sacred Heart. As St. Francis de Sales said, "Heart speaks to heart." Prayer does not conjure up God as rubbing a lamp conjures up a genie. The Holy Spirit is not a phantasm. We do not have that power over Him. His power is over us. He is always there waiting for our side of the correspondence. He never leaves us.

St. Paul writes to the Romans about prayer and encourages them in this divine correspondence. In that most beautiful passage, he writes, "For I am sure that neither death, nor life, nor angels, nor principalities, nor things present, nor things to come, nor powers, nor height, nor depth, nor anything else in all creation, will be able to separate us from the love of God in Christ Jesus our Lord" (Rom. 8:38–39). This is Paul—that compelling Jew who crosses the Mediterranean to teach people how to correspond with the God Who has corresponded with him.

Paul was, of course, a very different figure from the Victorian poet Elizabeth Barrett Browning. But she, too, corresponded with God. Her letters to her husband constitute some of the most lyrical love letters in all of English literature. The couple lived an idyllic life of about fourteen years in a sunny house in Florence. This glorious life, however, did not totally distract her from the joy of a higher love, of which her marriage was, to her, an intimation. As she writes in her lapidary sonnet:

> How do I love thee? Let me count the ways.
> I love thee to the depth and breadth and height
> My soul can reach, when feeling out of sight
> For the ends of being and ideal grace.
> I love thee to the level of every day's
> Most quiet need, by sun and candlelight.
> I love thee freely, as men strive for right.

She was writing to her husband, and she was also writing to her God since the sacrament of marriage is modeled on the divine correspondence of heavenly and earthly love. "To the depth and breadth and height my soul can reach": there is a mystical marriage between Christ and His Church. And the Church is the sacrament of that marriage—the historical evidence of the prayer between Christ and His Father in heaven. We participate in the inner prayer of the Holy Trinity by being baptized into Christ's Body, the Church.

The priest corresponds with the people by sharing this love of Christ for the flock. Now, we have human speech, and we're not all poets, and sometimes, when we try to describe it, we may say what's right, but we do not say it in the right way. I once read a description of the love of a priest for his people. It was in a document developed by an official Church commission. That commission's intention was thoroughly sound, and what it said was precisely right, but the way it described the love of a priest for the people was head-scratching. And I quote: "Pastoral charity constitutes the internal and dynamic principle capable of uniting the multiple and diverse pastoral activities of the priest and given the social-cultural and religious context in which he lives, is an indispensable instrument for drawing men to a life in grace."[6]

Thank God — literally — that Jesus did not describe His love to us in that way. On the shore of Galilee, Christ said to Peter, "Do you love Me? Feed My lambs. Do you love Me? Feed My sheep. Do you love Me? Feed My lambs" (see John 20:15–17). Jesus was praying to Peter! Peter, in turn, prayed to Christ: "Lord, you know that I love You." Recalling this poignant moment, Peter writes to the whole Church in his first letter — a prayer to the Church — about pastoral love. Peter's letter does not sound at all like that passage you just read. He says:

> So I exhort the elders among you, as a fellow elder and a witness of the sufferings of Christ as well as a partaker in the glory that is to be revealed. Tend the flock of God that is your charge, not by constraint but willingly, not for shameful gain but eagerly, not as domineering over those in your charge but being examples to the flock. And when the chief Shepherd is manifested you will obtain the unfading crown of glory. (1 Pet. 5:1–4)

---

[6] Congregation for the Clergy, *Directory on the Ministry and Life of Priests* (January 31, 1994), no. 43.

That is the correspondence of a saint, having corresponded with the Chief Shepherd on the shore of a lake, with the fellowship of saints. Without that correspondence, we do not live; we only exist. Our *Catechism* tells us that prayer is the memory of the Church brought to life by the Holy Spirit. Peter had much to remember —all his sins and offenses, his betrayal of Our Lord—and it could have haunted him into some dismal grave. But Our Lord ascended into heaven and gave him the Holy Spirit, that he might ever correspond with the Divine Love. He did not merely exist. He was not haunted by memory. He lived and was empowered by the memory of Christ. We can exist and be haunted by our past. Or we can live and be moved by past experience to the glory of heaven.

For a while there was a subway poster in New York City trying to stop, as much as a government can, promiscuity. And it said, "Anybody can make a baby. It takes a man to be a father." That's about as close to gospel theology as a bureaucracy will ever get. It is true: Anybody can make a baby. If we are only animals, we can biologically make a baby. But it takes an act of will to stay, to be faithful, to father. God willed to love us, and if we call upon Him by an act of the will, call upon Him as Our Father, then He manifests His Fatherhood to us and gives us life beyond existence. It takes grace, the power of the Holy Spirit, to understand how all this happens; for we live in a world that denies grace and wants us to think that all there is to life is existence.

In 1997, newspapers recorded the death of Jeanne Calment at the age of 122 in Arles, France—the oldest living human being. And she was as sharp as a tack. The reporter asked her, at 121, what her vision of the future was. She said, "Very brief." She had met Van Gogh. She had watched the building of the Eiffel Tower. For most of her adult life, she had a glass of wine with dinner. And her physician, on the occasion of her 121st birthday, told her to cut out the wine. Cut it out! When I read that, I thought, "Who is this medical genius? What's the point?" Cut out a glass of wine when you're 121! I think Our Blessed Lady would have said to that woman, "You are 121. Now it's time to have two glasses each night."

That would be totally in keeping with Our Blessed Lady at the wedding feast at Cana, when she saw that the wine of life had gone out and the guests had only water. By analogy, the joy of life was gone because people had stopped corresponding with God. So Our Lady turned to Jesus and did what only she could do. She perfectly corresponded with God. She spoke to her own Son. And He corresponded with her. "Woman, what is that between You and Me?" This is not the correspondence for which you were made and for which I came into the world. "My hour is not yet come" (see John 2:4). But it would come. On the Cross, wine became blood. The Eucharistic sacrifice happened, and Our Lady watched it happen. And in that divine correspondence between the Sacred Heart and the Immaculate Heart of a Woman, existence yielded to true life. And Our Lady reached up. She reached up to "the ends of being and ideal grace" and touched the cross.

Some evangelists say we need a personal relationship with Jesus — and it is true. But that requires qualification. That personal relationship is not a relationship between my id and my superego. It is not a feeling of sentiment within me. It is my contact with the True God. And that happens in full measure through the Holy Church, for the Church is born from the side of Christ when that blood flows down, flows down on the Lady, the Perfect Correspondent, the Help of All Christians in Prayer, the Mother, the Church.

Recently, in some areas of the United States there began a phenomenon of "mall churches" or "mega churches." Just as in the eighteenth century, when some churches were designed in the Baroque fashion to model opera houses, these churches were being fashioned after the cultural symbol of our decaying culture: the shopping mall. These churches had hairdressing shops, fast-food restaurants, and all kinds of services, and worship was nothing more than entertainment — soft rock bands and the like. The minister of one of these churches had gone to Europe to get some architectural ideas and saw the great cathedrals, but he rejected them all. He said they were not "user-friendly." Not user friendly? What is a church? Is it a theater? Is it to be friendly to the user? The Church is the house of living prayer. It is the place where we gather to offer the Holy Sacrifice through Christ in correspondence with the Eternal Father. It is not a user-friendly kind of a place. It is more than friendly. It is designed to make us fall to our knees, first of all, and to say that we are not worthy. But there are two obstacles to that kind of correspondence.

The first obstacle is a lack of faith. If we do not trust how God has spoken to mankind through His Church throughout all these ages, we will never understand that gift of awe at being able to speak to God through the Son of God, guided by the chief of our own race, our own Holy Mother.

The second obstacle is spiritual laziness, sloth — acedia, it is sometimes called. It is a lack of spiritual discipline, a reliance simply on feeling, on emotion. When that happens and the emotion then goes away, as it always does, we feel sad, our prayer is dry, and we become easily discouraged. There are times when our prayer will be dry. In our human nature, we will not be able to correspond perfectly with God. But if we are victims of this acedia, we will give up at that very moment. We have to do our part in the correspondence, for correspondence involves two people.

In the beautiful city of Bath, in England, is a tomb of a Bishop Montague who, in Elizabethan times, met a man on the street — Sir John Harrington, a godson of the irascible Queen Elizabeth I. It was raining. The bishop invited this man into the church. In that sad period of the split of the Church, called the Reformation, the abbey at Bath had been neglected. Big gaping holes punched through the roof, and, as the two men stood in the nave of the church, the water kept pouring down on them. Sir John said to the bishop, "Your grace, if the Church cannot save us from the waters above, how can she ever save us from the fires below?" The Church can save us from the fires below, but we, the Church Militant, have to fix the roof. In other words, we have to do our part in this earthly sphere, in time, in space, using every spiritual aid — the Rosary, special devotions — and also our intellect, our imagination, our will — in science and the arts — to manifest the voice of Christ corresponding with culture.

There are three stages to this correspondence, and they are modeled in that miracle of the draft of the fishes, when Our Lord stands on the shore and calls out to the Apostles, the fishermen in the boat. They have been fishing all night, says Scripture. That means, first of all, that our prayer has to be regular — not just when we feel like it, but constant, in season and out of season. We have to fish all night, and especially at night, when it seems dark and the correspondence seems a one-way conversation. Second, Our Lord tells the Apostles to cast their nets not on the left side but on the right side. Far from being a political commentary, Our Lord is saying that if you are going to enter into the mystical prayer of the Church, you have to change — change your own heart, reflect on what you have done so long as a routine, and let the Holy Spirit breathe into this conversation. So the nets are cast to the other side. If the Apostles had been fishing on the right side, He would have suggested that they cast their nets on the left! It is a sign of detachment, detachment from old ways, old expectations. We have to be prepared for an answer from God. And then, after the great draft of fish, Our Lord says, "Henceforth you will be fishers of men" (Matt. 4:19). And this points to the third stage. You see, they were fishermen, and He is not going to radically alter them. He is not making them carpenters. He is not making them governors or philosophers. They are going to be fishermen still. Only now they will fish for souls. To pray right, we have to cultivate the virtue proper to our own state in life—not trying to be something else, not trying to use the language of someone else, but using that prayer which is from the heart and conjoining it to the prayer of the Church which is always ours because it is the prayer of the family into which we have been reborn.

All this prayer comes to us from the wisdom of our Holy Mother, the Church. St. Paul says, "It is no longer I who live, but Christ who lives in me" (Gal. 2:20). And he writes this to us in a spiritual correspondence in his Letter to the Galatians.

In 1531, Our Holy Mother, the Perfect Correspondent with her Son, appeared in Guadalupe, in Mexico, and left her image on a tilma, a cloak of St. Juan Diego. Recent examination indicates that in the image there may very well be in the eye of Our Lady of Guadalupe the reflection of the figure, perhaps Juan Diego, seeing Our Blessed Lady for the first time, the one to whom the vision was vouchsafed. There is no explanation of how any artist could have forged that, not knowing the physics of how the eye receives an image. Yet we are all recorded in the eye of Our Mother. Mothers, after all, keep pictures of their children.

All through history, Our Mother has corresponded with us that way. She has kept our image in her eye, and every time we have prayed, she has been there to help us do it better. And, every time we have failed to pray, she has kept the prayer going on through all the saints who love her. And when we pray and feel that we are not doing it right, she is our Mother, telling us that it does not matter how we do it: it is the fact that we are doing it. If we feel that we are not doing it right, we are speaking as a child, and that is precisely what she wants. And our Mother, speaking as a Mother, will show us the Son, and the Son will show us the Father in Himself. I think even as we talk about prayer, the eyes of Our Lady must be twinkling and saying to us what she can say even more literally than St. Paul, "It is no longer I who live, but Christ who lives in me." In that image of Guadalupe, she is shown carrying the Holy Child in her womb. Our Lord does not appear visibly in that image, but it is in the womb that we know that He is to be found. We see Him when we see her. We see Christ when we see one another. And as we pray to God so reverently, we should speak to one another, knowing that each one of us is called to be part of this holy family, the Church, born of Christ's Blood on the Cross, and that all our prayer—our correspondence with God through Mary, Mediatrix of all grace—is offered through Him, with Him, and in Him.

Fire from Heaven and
the Making of Saints

I suppose I am not understating the situation to suggest that many schoolchildren have never heard of Iapetus or Clymene or Prometheus. They are figures from Greek mythology. Nor, I suspect, is it understating things to suggest that most schoolchildren today have not been told there is even such a thing as Greek mythology. Greek mythology serves a useful purpose — separating reality from myth, fact from fiction. But, without a knowledge of it, a child risks growing up thinking *everything* is mythology because the child has never learned to distinguish the two. The child begins to think that there are no facts.

Mythology is an attempt to begin with a theory and illustrate it with a fictional story. Christian theology is not mythology. Christian theology begins with the story, which is real, and then tries to extrapolate facts from this real story. Greek myths illustrate human theories about human nature. Christian theology declares the facts of human nature in the light of the divine nature. Theology then opens us to the endless attempt of the human mind to fathom the deep mysteries that God shows about Himself and about us.

In the acutely psychological myth, Prometheus appears on the scene born of Iapetus, who is a Titan, and Clymene, who is a sea nymph. So, right from the start, you know Prometheus is not your ordinary man on the street. But he is a man, nonetheless, an advocate for the human race. He takes fire from the god of the gods, Zeus, or Jupiter, as the Romans knew him, or sometimes Jove. We take his name rightfully in vain when we say "by Jove." But this was a mythical god, this Zeus, and he is so jealous that his fire had been stolen that he punishes Prometheus by taking the fire back into his heavenly kingdom. Whereupon Prometheus enlists the help of the goddess of wisdom, Minerva, and goes up into heaven, and you can see where this is going. Wisdom is appropriated by man to enter heaven.

This is a recurring myth in our culture. There are those who think that with adequate intellectual help, we, too, can live with the gods. Prometheus does get into the imperium, the heavenly height, and steals fire from the sun. Zeus is still mighty Zeus, and he takes his own revenge. He tries to seduce Prometheus by the first of all the women of the race, Pandora.

Pandora is given a box that holds all the world's ills. Now, she is a woman, and women are as inquisitive as men. So she opens the box, and all the perplexities of the world are let loose, and all that remains in the box is hope. While she is supposed to seduce Prometheus and bring his downfall, Prometheus meanwhile has been consorting with the goddess of wisdom. He sees through this whole charade, you see. And so instead of wedding her, what does he do? He has his brother Epimetheus marry her instead. Zeus is once again angry. Nothing has gone according to plan. Epimetheus, not Prometheus, has married Pandora. So once again, Prometheus is punished. This time, Vulcan, the god of the fires, the forger of armor, the forger of chains — where, by the way, we get the term "vulcanize" — chains Prometheus to Mount Caucasus, where vultures feed upon his liver. And to ensure that this is a never-ending suffering, as the liver is consumed, it grows back again, and the vultures keep eating.

Eventually Prometheus, rescued by all Western culture, expresses the attempt of man to soar with the gods through the use of tricks and the use of wisdom and the appropriation of energy — of power, of something possessed by the gods themselves. This is the direct opposite of the Christian fact.

God is a jealous God only in the sense that He does not want to lose us. He is the veritable God; He is not a mythical god. And so, He is not insecure about Himself. God is God, and man is man. God is not a half god, nor is man a superman. The Promethean myth holds that man can become superman. In our culture, some of the actors who portrayed Superman have bedazzled through special effects and have almost convinced us that this impossible dream is, in fact, possible. The irony is that, in real life, many of the actors who played Superman have met tragic ends. One, George Reeves, allegedly committed suicide. Another one, Christopher Reeve, was paralyzed in an equestrian riding event, and though he valiantly struggled to deal with the resulting suffering, he died in 2004, shortly after turning fifty-two. He, you, and I are *human*; we are not *superhuman*.

When we begin to believe the Promethean myth, our civilization begins to quake. Civilization is based on the cooperation of people. According to an economy of mutual obligations, when certain people in civilization aspire to be supermen, other people become their slaves — philosophically, economically, ideologically, sociologically.

Every culture has to have air breathed into it to understand why it exists apart from mere economics or politics or sociology. And that is how we get something deeper than civilization. That is how we get culture. As "civilization" comes from the word meaning "city" — the ability to live together — "culture" comes from the word "cult," meaning how we worship.

A culture gives life to a civilization by offering it a god — an object of truth to which that civilization consecrates itself. A civilization, St. John Paul II reminded us, should be a civilization of love. But within that civilization, a culture can build up that militates against love. Love gives life. But if a culture worships death, then it becomes a "culture of death," as St. John Paul II so aptly dubbed it, because it knows nothing beyond the morgue.

What does it mean to worship death? Are we pagans who worship false gods? Yes! And those false gods of death are what we call the seven deadly sins: pride, anger, lust, avarice, gluttony, envy, and sloth. And by this false worship, a population disintegrates. We are barely at replacement level, numerically, in terms of population in the United States right now. Western civilization is on the brink of economic disaster because of a contraceptive and an abortive mentality. But those mentalities are rooted in a deadlier kind of worship. It is the worship of the superman. "I want to be me. I have the right to do with *my own body* what I will. I can choose what I want."

We can choose, but the choice has always been placed before us by the true God this way: choose life or choose death! Choose the true God or go back to the gods of our ancestors—all of those malignant, pedantic, venal symbols of mythology. This is a question of attitude. Real attitude, not the superficial attitude we speak of every day. I go through many airports, and in one airport I noticed a shoeshine stand with a sign that said, "Shine $3.00; Supershine $4.00." I asked the proprietor of that stand what the difference was, and he said, "Attitude." There is an attitude that chooses life, which makes the difference between the ordinary shine and the supershine. And it's called holiness. But there is also an attitude of death, which is the difference between the life that God has given us and the illusion we would rather live.

We live in a world in which people want to steal fire from heaven. They want to take the energy of God, as they perceive it, to use for their own ends: self-hypnosis, political placebos, government systems, New Age religion, anything that will persuade the mind of man that God is nothing other than an energy that can become our own. Prometheus furtively stole fire from heaven because Zeus did not want him to have it. How different from the way the true God acts toward us. When Jesus comes into the world, His cousin, John the Baptist, says, "I baptize you with water for repentance, but he who is coming after me ... will baptize you with the Holy Spirit and with fire" (Matt. 3:11). When Christ comes into the world He says, "I came to cast fire upon the earth; and would that it were already kindled!" (Luke 12:49). He does not want to hide fire from us. His whole point in coming to the world is to bring fire to us, and it is the fire of truth, of love, and the fire of His own Holy Spirit. And that fire destroys as well as gives life.

People may ask, "How can a loving God bring fire to the earth? It destroys." It is because He is a God of love, and wherever there is love, His heavenly fire will destroy hate. He is the God of truth, and whenever the fire of truth comes into the world, it will destroy lies. We worship this truth through the power of the Holy Spirit, who descended with tongues of fire upon the Apostles. And when we go into a church, we worship this Holy Spirit in holiness and in truth—not as supermen but confessing anything but—that we are sinful men, that we are sinful women, that we are sinful children, and that we are nothing without God. And with God, we are not supermen. We are more than that. Our Holy Lady, the chief of the race, is not a superwoman. She, like all of us, is a human, a little lower than the angels. But because of Her obedience to the fire of heaven, she is the Queen of the angels as well as of men. That is why we should have a holy aura when we go into the temple of God.

And what has happened to the temple of God in our culture? It is the Catholic Church, commissioned by God to spread the fullness of truth to all the world, that shows the world what it is to be in a holy place in the presence of the living God.

A Crisis in Culture

But Prometheus has entered even the Catholic churches. Prometheus has declared himself superman. Prometheus has said, turn the altars on himself, the prayers on himself. Even his hymns speak of himself instead of God. What is the temple of superman? It is a living room. Some churches have been redecorated with wall-to-wall carpeting, potted plants, and even, horror of horrors, electric candles! Prometheus does not want to offer God a full sacrifice. He wants to have his cake and eat it too. At the very most, he will offer his God an electric candle, but he will control the switch, because Prometheus has stolen the fire from heaven. Go into some of our churches today and see how they reflect our Promethean culture. What have we done to these churches? They look like ecclesiastical Chernobyls. They represent the meltdown of Christian consciousness. These are temples of life, but they speak only of cultural death.

Prometheus does not use humble language such as *quaesumus*, *deprecemur*, *obsequium* — those words of the Roman rite expressing humility, unworthiness, and prostration before God. Prometheus wants to erase such language. He does not even want to kneel. He wants us to go to conventions. He wants to bring the nations together at these conventions and declare that we now are the gods of the earth. We can control population. We can decide when life begins and when that life should end. We tried it in the United Nations conference in Cairo and in Beijing and so on. But it is a mythical conundrum — unfortunately, a deadly myth.

No, the fire from heaven does not make us supermen; it makes us saints.

I was asked to give a talk to some officials of the United Nations shortly after another theologian had spoken to them. He was rather prominent in saying that the pope and the Catholic Church are wrong about many things.

I did not want to get involved in those polemics. So I simply announced that I would speak on the topic "Can an Ambassador

Be a Saint?" To my surprise the hall was filled, and to my greater surprise, I was asked back.

Organizations such as the United Nations have their functions, but they become self-destructive and forget that man is called to holiness—nothing less, and nothing more. And if man thinks there is something more, he will destroy himself. God is the God of life—the life that he plants in our intellect, our imagination, and in our will. The Sacrifice of the Mass is the offering of the Lord of life on our behalf. Every Mass is our entrance into heaven. If we are Prometheus in church, that makes no sense. All we want to do is steal heaven and bring it here and keep it as our possession.

I was in the sacristy of a church I was visiting on one occasion when I heard behind me the click of high heels—sometimes a dangerous sound in a sacristy. The lady who had entered told me that she was to be the lector that day and she wanted to know what the theme of the liturgy was for the day. I was rather taken aback. I said, "There is only one theme of the liturgy, and that's the Death and Resurrection of Jesus Christ." At the beginning of the Mass, she announced that I was the celebrant, or "presider," as she called me, and then announced that the theme of the Mass was "the Death and Resurrection of Jesus Christ."

Well, at least she did get that right. But our culture does not get it right. It has forgotten its own theme, and when it forgets the theme of life, it misses the truth of life and the beauty of life. A venerable architect in this century, Ralph Adams Cram, said truth is not beauty, beauty, truth; as has sometimes vainly been said. But there is a connection. And truth always reveals itself in beauty, whether in conduct, art, philosophy, or religion, and everyone intuitively understands that something ugly is a lie.

St. Thomas Aquinas said that beauty is whatever pleases. But it was a saint speaking that, and what he meant is *whatever pleases a saint.* Otherwise you are speaking of superficial aestheticism. "Real beauty consists," he said, "of right proportion, order, and clarity." Right proportion is the gift of the virtue of faith, which understands God and man in relation to God. Order is the gift of the virtue of hope. Unless we see the order of the world, we have no hope. But even Pandora had some hope left in her little carrying case.

And clarity is the gift of the virtue of love. Unless we see God, who made us, as perfect love, all life will be obscured to us. When that happens, we cannot worship. We worship God in faith, in love, in hope, and the beauty of holiness. And when people begin to doubt the power of God's grace to transform us, when they begin to question whether His fire can really give us life, then they shrink away from God; they begin to fear Him. Puritans did that, and a group of Catholic puritans did that too: they were called the Jansenists, and they keep cropping up in every culture of death. In the eighteenth century in France, these Jansenists tried to destroy the liturgy because they did not want saints and statues to remind us of the beauty of holiness. Imagine! They did not want the solemn ritual to remind us of the dance of heaven. They did not want the Latin language to remind us of the universality of the faith. They did not want the cult of the Sacred Heart to display the flames of God's own love. They did not want the priests at the altar saying secret prayers because they did not want to know that we could intercede with heaven to a God who sometimes wants us there.

In the archdiocese of Lyons, Archbishop Antoine de Malvin de Montazet began to deconstruct the liturgy that way in the name of this romantic minimalism. His successor, Antoine Adrien Lamourette, did the same thing; he tried to remove the crucifix from the great cathedral of Lyons. And the respected Bishop Jacques-Bénigne Bossuet had a nephew, the bishop of Troyes, who tried to purify the liturgy, as he saw it, by going back to primitive sources. But the only sources that he consulted were those he imagined were part of the primitive youth of the Church. His metropolitan archbishop reminded him, "You are creating an illusion. God's fire breathes into His Church through the developing tradition of the liturgy, and we are, from time to time, to reform it, but not to replace it."

Prometheus wants to replace the liturgy; he does not want to reform it. And if we try, like Prometheus, to reconstruct some powerful liturgy that we imagine gave breath and life to the liturgy as it was in the old days, we will not end up with the court of heaven; we will end up with a liturgical Disneyland.

The last sixty years have seen a 60 percent decline in attendance at the Holy Mass, partly because people, seeing what has been done to the Mass, have lost heart and also because people have begun to become Prometheus again in the Church and worship themselves instead of their God. Pope Pius V reformed the liturgy, as did Clement VIII, Urban VIII, Pius X, John XXIII — it goes on and on. But they did not intend the replacement of the liturgy. Terrible mistakes have been made by liturgical Prometheans over the years. May these mistakes not happen again.

The Reality of Christianity

Jonathan Swift was a clergyman in the eighteenth century, probably best known as the author of *Gulliver's Travels*. He was a master of English letters and a man who enjoyed considerable prestige. In his study one day, engrossed in writing, he heard a tumult outside and inquired as to its cause. Told that the people had gathered to watch an eclipse of the sun, he instructed his servant to inform them that, in fact, the dean had postponed the eclipse for two days. The crowd dispersed.

A man with such authority should be listened to, but not on matters of religion. While he was a master of English letters, Swift was not much a master of Religion. He was a deist. He believed in God, but he did not understand quite how God was connected with the world and how the world was connected with God. God had made the world and then had sort of vanished and left it to its own devices. That is how Swift saw things. But that same man knew enough about religion to say that there are people in this world who have enough religion to hate but not enough to love. He was speaking of religion as that binding element—for the word comes from the Latin word *religare*, which means "to bind." That is to say, it brings laws and moral perception together in a philosophy of living as well as an account of how we are to live, why we live, and Who has given us life.

A Crisis in Culture

There have been countless religions, and it would demean all of them to say that they have all been the same. Were that true, we would not have to speak of them in the plural. It would patronize religions and their founders to say that they are equally true, which is a polite way of saying that they are equally wrong.

Christianity, on the other hand, is not a religion, not in the most profound sense. Christianity is what comes at the end of all religious striving. Some religions, better than others, have perceived the existence of God and have interpreted the world's relation to Him. But all religions have failed, on their own, to understand what God tells us in Christ. Christ speaks of the true religion given by the True God by His Chosen People when He says, "Think not that I have come to abolish the law and the prophets; I have come not to abolish them but to fulfil them" (Matt. 5:17). He is the Law. He is the God Who speaks through the prophets. He is the God Whom the law serves. He is the God of Whom all the prophets speak. And the last prophet, John the Baptist, announced, and I paraphrase, "There is now to come into the world, One greater than any prophet." Our Lord does not destroy religion. He lets us know that the quest of religion now is answered in Him, the Lord of the world.

If we understand religion only as a binding, we will think that in order to live as free and independent people with a life that is lived to the full, we must liberate ourselves from religion. People who have done that in our day are called secularists. The Latin word *saeculum* roughly means an encompassing period of time or a long existence. The first secularizers were sophisticates, well informed of this world, and most of them probably would not have taken umbrage at being called secularists. It would be very strange indeed to call ourselves "eating-ists" simply because we spend much of the day eating. We know that it is wrong to be called a racist simply because we belong to a particular race. Foolish then, is it not, for anyone, simply by virtue of the fact that he lives in the world, to call himself a secularist.

The secularist does not understand how the world works because he is trying to separate the world from the world's God. Our Lord says in the fifth chapter of John, "My Father is working still, and I am working" (John 5:17). The deist was limited. God did not make the world only to leave it. Our Lord transfigures the world. He goes to the top of a mountain and is transfigured in glory Himself. He does not become an angel; he does not become a Mithraic bull or a Druidical tree. He is still Christ, the man and God. Grace does not destroy nature but perfects it. The light comes from within Christ, and we see human glory ever more clearly in the light of divinity.

Secularism is the world acting without reference to its God. That is theoretical madness, just the way natural psychosis consists in individual behavior without reference to people around the self. It is the secularist who is vague. It is the secularist who does not get the world right. The secularist thinks he is a pragmatist, but he is living an illusion. The illusory perception says there is no God, there is no truth, and by so believing, the secularist also fails to see the prince of lies. That is precisely what the prince of lies wants. He does not want us to see him, for his power is derivative. He has control over this world to the extent that we fail to perceive him in his wiles and his ways. This is why so-called sophisticated people seem so very blind to palpable evidence.

The twentieth century was an open textbook of the unreality of the secularist. This is why the twentieth century was such a playground for the prince of lies.

I remember as if it were yesterday being at a house in England that had once been the property of the native Virginian, Lady Astor—Nancy Astor, a viscountess and the first female Member of Parliament. In the 1920s and 1930s she held an eclectic little court of celebrities, intellectuals, and political figures at Cliveden, her stately country home in Buckinghamshire. They gathered there regularly to discuss various social and political events of the day. They were confident of their worldly wisdom. So deluded were they that they failed to see a cloud rising on the horizon. Oh, they knew there was trouble over there in Germany—trouble they said was rooted in economic policy. They said that the army being formed over there was a political strategy—that that man over there named Hitler was just another politician. They thought they could solve this problem with compromise, with appeasement. After all, they knew the world and the world's ways, and they knew how you could broker a certain peace. One man, though, who frequently sat in that library with the so-called Cliveden Set, told them they were wrong. Winston Churchill, as he sat there with a cigar in one hand and a brandy in the other, could never be mistaken for a desert mystic. Nor was he a secularist. He was a man of natural virtue in the classical order, at least in sufficient amount to know from history and from his own experience that there is good and that there is evil and that what was going on across the channel was not just economic, not just political, not just the functioning of a charismatic politician. It was palpable "evil," as he said, calling it by its name. And for me to say Mass in that very room on the spot where those conversations took place, to offer the Holy Sacrifice of Christ, who won the ultimate battle over evil and death, was particularly moving.

Our world has paid a great price for the unreality of the secularist. We have suffered much because of the gossamer unworldliness of the worldly. In his encyclical *Centesimus Annus*, Pope St. John Paul II mentioned the Yalta Conference, which bartered much of Eastern Europe for the sake of peace with Stalin and the Marxists. At the end of the conference, back in Washington, Franklin Roosevelt was asked by an aide if he had possibly given away the store to Stalin? Roosevelt replied, "Remember, Stalin was once a seminarian. And I think that if you scratch him on the surface, you'll find a *gentleman* underneath."

That was the voice of sophistication. And it was dead wrong! The blood of a generation cries out to us just how wrong he was. For we now know that if you scratched the surface of Stalin, what you found was not a gentleman but the devil. Apropos of which, a friend of mine reminded me of a line in Shakespeare's *King Lear*: "The prince of darkness is a gentleman." Satan knows enough about the secularist to realize that the secularist would recognize him if he wore red flannel pajamas and carried a pitchfork. Instead, he goes to his cocktail parties in his best cocktail attire, his dinner jacket, and speaks eloquently in his parliaments, and writes very sophisticated-sounding legal opinions in the supreme courts of the world. He knows how to deal with the naïveté of the secularist. The secularist wants to be a gentleman in a gentleman's world. So, Satan will pretend to be a gentleman.

In short, the secularist misreads creation in two basic ways. The first is by suspecting creation. The secularist in this school can never be quite certain of what portends in the world. The world is a threat; the world is corrupt and can only be manipulated and controlled. And we can find peace in it only by an eternal suspicion about our own nature. This was the motive of the Puritans and the motive of the Catholic Puritans — the Jansenists — of whom we have spoken.

There was a synod in Pistoia, Italy, in 1786. Bishop Scipione de' Ricci, a Jansenist, proposed guidelines for changing the Mass, and they sounded very much like some more recent proposals. Ricci did not really understand the generosity of God's grace — offering Himself freely in a true sacrifice for those who will receive Him. Ricci did not understand the majesty of the Church's language, which transcends ordinary speech. He did not want Latin. He did not trust the ability of the priest to transcend that divide between the world and heaven through secret prayers. He did not want to be reminded that there are saints in heaven praying for us, so he wanted to eliminate statues. All of this was condemned a few years later by Pope Pius VI in the bull *Auctorem Fidei* (1794).

In various ways, pseudo-religious ways sometimes, this hatred of creation betrays the secularist's misunderstanding of God's grace. And how does God answer it? Through the sacraments. The sacraments are the prime declaration that grace does not destroy nature but perfects it. God saves us through things. If we are a secularist, we will not understand it. It has always been hard to understand. Our Lord said, "Unless you eat the flesh of the Son of Man and drink his blood, you have no life in you" (John 6:53). And the crowd walked away. This is a hard saying.

"Will you also go away?" He asks His own men. And Peter replies for all the Apostles, as Peter is always replying through the ages though the popes, his successors, "Lord, to whom shall we go? You have the words of eternal life" (John 6:67–68). Yes, however it happens, whatever happens, we will recognize, we will discern Your Body and Your Blood.

This is the real sophistication of religious striving. If only 23 percent of all self-proclaimed Catholics of the United States discern the Real Presence of Christ in the Eucharist, it is because even in the Church, secularism has gotten wrong the world and the God Who made this world.

The other mistake of the secularist, if he's not going to suspect and, indeed, hate creation, is to idolize it. He builds myriad idolatries in this secular religiosity. Rationalism worships the reason within creation. Humanism worships the human race itself, as though it were God. Sensualism worships feelings. Indifferentism worships ambiguity. Nature mysticism, speciesism, and radical ecologism worship things as though they were their own creators. This religiosity does not discern the hierarchy of being, does not differentiate between the death of the baby seal and the death of a human baby. All because it has gotten the world, and the God Who made this world, wrong.

The answer to this idolatry is the Resurrection. St. Paul writes in his First Letter to the Corinthians, in the fifteenth chapter, "If I offer myself in the arena to the animals at Ephesus purely for human motive" — if I'm willing to die just for a secular statement — "it's only human bravado. What good is it? Then I become just like those voices mentioned in the book of the prophet Isaiah, saying, 'Eat, drink, and be merry for tomorrow we die'" (see 1 Cor. 15:32; Isa. 22:13). A kind of panache bravado, but ultimately tragic.

But if we understand that the world was made by God, we do not have to have a tragic finale. We will understand that we were made to live with God forever. And then we will be able to say supernaturally, not in contradiction with nature, but in revelation of the whole purpose of nature, "Death is swallowed up in victory! O death, where is thy victory? O death where is thy sting?" (1 Cor. 15:55). It is a wonderful hymn frozen on the lips of the secularist. As the secularist is so unworldly about the world, so the Christian, by living the fulfillment of all religious striving, is the most sophisticated about this world. Only the Christian can really pray as the secularist cannot pray *in saecula saeculorum*, "to the end of all the worlds, to the end of all ages of ages." This is our eternal happiness: not to escape from this world but to live and serve God in this world so that we may be with Him forever. God is our eternal happiness, and He makes us happy in this world.

St. Teresa of Avila said, "All the way to heaven is heaven." That's not a contradiction of the world; it is an explanation of it.

Judge Robert Bork, as a legal philosopher, commenting on some opinions from certain Supreme Court justices, said they gave the impression that the right to free speech is no longer ordered to the pursuit of truth but only to the pursuit of happiness. That free speech, in other words, should not be regulated by how it obeys the truths of this world, but simply how it pleases others by the very utterance. That kind of sensuality demeans the human race, demeans nature, ignores natural law. This is how we enter into a culture of death. And even the secularist who does not like that language uses euphemisms, admitting that we are in a culture of death. He will talk about the extinction of species. He is really afraid of his own extinction. In one breath, he will talk about a nuclear winter, and, in another breath, he will talk about global warming. These are all signs of a deep fear that someday we will have nothing braver to say than "Eat, drink, and be merry for tomorrow we die."

Our society is in moral crisis, it is clear. The prophets have long said it; and at the end of all prophecies, Our Lord declared it. And now we are living it most vividly on a grand scale. *Newsweek*, in a survey in the late twentieth century, found that 83 percent of all Americans acknowledged that we are in a moral breakdown in this culture. Today, one suspects the number would be as high, if not higher. As an experiment, I opened the *New York Times* one day on an airplane and counted how many deep moral questions were posed, albeit unintentionally, by the editor. On the front page was an article about the New York City Council's decision to rezone the Times Square area, where in an eight-block radius there are about 450 pornographic businesses. The head of the American Civil Liberties Union has said that to shut down these businesses would be to deprive New York City of its rich cultural tradition. Then there was an announcement of a play opening on Broadway in which a woman plays a man playing a woman. Next was an article about the late Mr. Fidel Castro paying a visit to the editorial offices of that newspaper to thank them for the support they had given him in his revolution. Next, an article about "trash talk" on television and what could be done about it. Then, the article about the increasing legal problems concerning malpractice suits involving cases of AIDS deaths. Next, a full-page paid advertisement by a couple of Hollywood producers letting statesmen in our country know, "You talk about a breakdown of family values and the corruption of the entertainment industry. We have finally produced a film which upholds family values and believes that there are certain things that are so right, that they are always right." They were right. St. Thomas Aquinas would have been pleased to read that ad, as would St. Augustine—to say nothing of the Lord of all creation. Yet they had to pay for it to be said, since our analysis of it in journals such as the *New York Times* is so unsophisticated because of our deluded secularism; we do not know what people in their plaintive desperation are longing for. People want happiness in this world, but they will find it only if they are sophisticated enough in the name of Christ to know that He is the source of our happiness.

When Pope St. John Paul II came to the United Nations, he went into the meditation room, where there is nothing but a rock, and he stood in front of it. He did not say anything; he did not have to. The picture said everything. That rock is just a pebble, but *he* is the rock. Peter is the rock upon which Christ founded the Church, and it is in the Church that we understand the meaning of this world and the God of this world—that God comes into this world and says what no human institution can say: "Peace I give to you; not as the world gives do I give to you" (John 14:27).

The Battle for Holiness

Symbols represent facts that are too wonderful and too terrible for easy speech. That is why we use them. To dismiss them as only symbolic is very wrong. Take, for example, the extraordinary symbol at the beginning of the Bible. It is a sword. Far from being a mere symbol, it represents the horror and the glory of the entire human adventure. Adam and Eve were cast out of Paradise, as you might recall, and a sword of fire was set up. It was a symbol. Adam and Eve could not regain Paradise on their own. The recovery of Paradise could happen only through the use of a sword in battle.

And how was that to happen? After many centuries, Our Lord came into the world, and He climbed the hill we call the Mount of the Beatitudes. And He said, "Blessed are the poor.... Blessed are the meek.... Blessed are those who mourn.... Blessed are those who thirst for justice.... Blessed are the merciful.... Blessed are the pure.... Blessed are the peacemakers.... Blessed are those who are persecuted for righteousness sake." This was the battle strategy. It seems strange to say, but Our Lord on that hill was outlining the great campaign for the battle that would regain Paradise, and it would involve a sword.

A few years later, on another mountain, really nothing more than a hill, Our Lord hangs on the Cross, and on that same hill of Calvary is His Mother, watching Him. There, she is, the incarnation of the Beatitudes, even as He is the Incarnation of God Himself. For she is all the things that He described on the mountain. And all the things that He described on that mountain are necessary for a battle. She will be part of this combat. She, above all others, is poor. She has given up all that was hers so that she might follow the will of her Lord. She is the embodiment of weakness: "Let it be done to me according to Your word" (see Luke 1:38). She is the Mother of all who mourn. She is mourning there at the foot of the Cross for the world's greatest loss. She thirsts for justice even as she watches her Son unjustly being made to thirst on the Cross. She is merciful. She is merciful to her Son by staying with Him. She is merciful to Him as she listens to Him cry for mercy shown to His persecutors. She shows us what purity means. She is the ultimate peacemaker, for she brings the Prince of Peace into the world through her body. And who can deny that she is persecuted as she stands there for those miserable three hours?

How can this all be part of the battle?

A soldier has to be poor. He goes onto the battlefield with nothing but his uniform, which has been given him, and the weapon in his hand. He has to be meek, for he has to obey orders. He has to know about mourning because he is surrounded by corpses, and he may very well end up one of them. A soldier in battle knows what thirst is and, according to the code of chivalry, knows what mercy is. A true soldier has to embody purity, for he has to have a pure cause for which to fight. He has to be a peacemaker, for that is what all just war is meant to attain. And he will know, as the battle begins, what it means to be persecuted.

Our Lady embarks upon this titanic struggle, along with Her Son, on the top of that hill. It is the fulfillment, the fact, that the Sermon on the Mount of the Beatitudes symbolized. Our Lady is not an angel. She is the Queen of Angels, but she's a woman. Blaise Pascal—the French Catholic theologian, writer, physicist, mathematician, and inventor, who knew human nature — said, centuries ago, that he who wants to play the angel becomes a beast. People who think they are angelic do not know the human condition, and they bring many sorrows into the world.

We are engaged in a struggle that is human. But because it is human, it has to be supernatural because we are God's creatures. When something goes wrong in the human condition, it is a sure sign that we have been dislocated from our supernatural destiny. Any attempt to recover Paradise as a purely humanitarian effort will simply let beasts loose in the world — not unlike what we experienced in the summer of 2020. And looking back to the prior century, with the perspective of time, we can see quite clearly how that has played out.

Karl Marx said that the human struggle was economic. Sigmund Freud said that the human struggle enlisted the subconscious, the subconscious fact of the human disorder. Give them some credit. At least they recognized a battle was being waged. If we try to be angels, we will turn a blind eye to the battle altogether and open the field to the enemy.

As in the twentieth century, and every other century, we are presently engaged in a palpable spiritual warfare. That does not mean that it is less than human. It means that the battle space of the human condition is far fiercer than any battle fought in the political order.

On October 25, 1854 — a month and a half before Pius IX's December 8 affirmation of the dogma of the Immaculate Conception of Our Lady — the famous Battle of Balaclava was fought during the Crimean War. Now, we are familiar with the story of "The Charge of the Light Brigade" that took place during it. "Half a league, half a league,/ Half a league onward." It has written itself into the indelible lore of military tragedy and heroism. What happened in the Charge of the Light Brigade was that the British, facing Russian opponents armed with some 10,000 armed men, had a confusion in their orders. Lord Ragland gave instructions to a Lord Lucan, who misinterpreted them. He thought that he was being commanded to order the *charge* of the Light Brigade. And so he did, prompting Lord Cardigan to take a deep breath before leading his men into a veritable "valley of death," given the over-whelming odds against them. Ten thousand armed Russian troops against 673 British troops. Within minutes, 247 British soldiers lay dying. French General Pierre François Joseph Bosquet saw the entire scene and uttered those poignant words, "C'est magnifique, mais ce n'est pas la guerre: c'est de la folie" (It is magnificent, but it is not war. It is madness).

The struggle called human history has been magnificent and has produced magnificent characters, magnificent personalities, magnificent inventions, magnificent civilizations. But unless it has engaged itself spiritually, unless the human adventure has un-derstood that the ultimate battle is for the regaining of Paradise, it is not really war at all. It may be heroic on the human level, but it is not heroic on the spiritual level, which is where the battle for our human identity is engaged and where it is defined. For holiness is the life of the virtues lived heroically, at full force, for a supernatural end.

Our Lord on the Cross was fighting a battle. He suffered sorrows recounted in the Sorrowful Mysteries of the Holy Rosary. Our Lady was part of the battle, and she had her sorrows too—traditionally, Seven Sorrows: the sorrows that Our Lord suffers as she sees them through her immaculate eyes.

The battle in which all this sorrow took place began with a sword, and it happened in the Temple in Jerusalem. We know that Our Lady and St. Joseph took the holy Child there to dedicate Him to God according to the rabbinical law. St. Augustine says that Our Lady carried Jesus, but the fact was that Jesus was carrying Mary.

For He is her God as well as our God. He had been predestined for this moment, and He had planned for her to bring Him into His Father's house. This is the good news that Mary tells us. She serves her own Lord by carrying Him. And all the while, she finds that He is carrying her, and that is the fact of how God behaves with each one of us when we participate in His battle. Similarly, all we have to do is be available to Him, to serve Him, to be willing to carry Him through history, and we find that He is carrying us. As we engage Satan in spiritual combat, there are times that we may seem to be doing it alone, but Our Lord is there sustaining us on the battlefield.

"But standing by the cross of Jesus were his mother, and his mother's sister," St. John wrote (John 19:25). This is the only mention of Mary in the Battle of the Passion. And that is all that St. John has to say because that is how she fights the battle, just by being there. In the same way, in the second chapter of his Gospel, St. John says, "On the third day there was a marriage at Cana in Galilee, and the mother of Jesus was there" (John 2:1). She is always there. And that is the beginning of military preparation.

It really is the common sense of any military strategy. When the trumpet call is given, the troops have to be present. The trumpet call is given on Mount Calvary, Our Lord is present, inescapably on the Cross, and His Mother is there at the foot. So the battle begins. We begin to understand now, slowly, what that sword in Eden was all about. How many times does that sword show up, reminding us that we are far from Paradise! Our Lord comes into the world, and many swords in the name of the loss of Paradise are flashed at the massacre of the Innocents. At the Last Supper, the Apostles produced two swords, prompting Our Lord to say, "Enough." In the Garden of Our Lord's agony, Peter takes a sword and cuts off the ear of the Jewish high priest's servant Malchus.

Our Lord tells Peter to put away his sword. For now, they are entering into a deeper battle of which these swords are going to be tokens. The real sword is going to be that sword that flamed at the Garden of Eden. On the Cross, Our Lord cries out, "Father, forgive them; for they know not what they do" (Luke 23:34). And suddenly in the mind of the Virgin, there had to come alive again the words that she heard when she took the Baby into the Temple in Jerusalem. Because when she had done that, carrying Our Lord but really being carried by Him, remember that the old man Simeon said to her that one day a sword would pierce her heart as well (Luke 2:35). And when Our Lord says, "Father, forgive them"—forgive these people who are killing Him—certainly the sword begins to pierce her heart. It was hard for Our Lord to say that from the Cross because His mouth was so dry and caked with blood. But it was far harder for her to hear because it was her Son and she was suffering for Him. And she could see the cruelty of those around her at the foot of the Cross doing this to Him, and in her purity, their viciousness was only magnified, making it that much crueler.

It is hard to forgive, but that is part of the battle as well. Elie Wiesel won the Nobel Peace Prize for the work he did after the Second World War on behalf of Jewish refugees, in which he starkly reminded the world of the horrors of the concentration camps, in which he had once been a prisoner. On January 26, 1995, the day before the fiftieth anniversary of the liberation of Auschwitz, he said something that I would reluctantly have to say was not something Our Lord would have said. Reluctantly because I have never been in a concentration camp, reluctantly because I do not bear that great burden of suffering that Mr. Wiesel or his people bore. But in that speech at that ungodly place in southern Poland, he said with great indignation, "Please, God, do not have mercy on those who created this place. God of forgiveness do not forgive those murderers of Jewish children here. Do not forgive the murderers and their accomplices." The blood seemed to be crying out from the ground. And everyone who has lived the battle of human life can sympathize with that voice. But it is not the voice we hear from the Cross.

In another concentration camp, Ravensbrück, in northern Germany, there was found a note after the liberation of the camp. And that note, the author of which we do not know, except to say it was one of the prisoners, read: "Lord, remember not only those of good will but also those of ill will. Here we learn courage and forbearance. May the fruits we have borne be for their forgiveness." A line like that is the beginning of a victory—the victory not of an ordinary battle, in which we seek revenge, but of a supernatural battle, the great battle of life in which we fight with another weapon: a sword of mercy. It is only with supernatural help and divine grace that we are able to say what that letter said.

There are three kinds of rebellion against Paradise. And they are summed up in the story Our Lord told in the parable of the man who gave a banquet and invited guests, each of whom had an excuse why he could not attend (Luke 14:15–24).

One man said that he had just bought a farm. And here we find our first rebellion against God's invitation to Paradise—the world. The second man said he had just married a wife. And here is revealed that the second way we rebel against God is through the flesh, not through the sacramental offering of holy union in marriage, but with a preoccupation with the flesh and distractions in the name of love—love, which is supposed to make us servants of God but if wrongly ordered makes us rebels. The third man said that he had just bought a yoke of oxen. The third obstacle to Paradise, then, is power—that desire to control. And so we have a triad, that classical triad—the world, the flesh, and the devil, the prince of pride and human power. That is the enemy in the spiritual warfare.

And ultimately, at the root of the corruption of the world and the flesh and power in all its forms is diabolical pride. Pride refuses to show mercy because pride is an illusion in itself and knows how weak it is. King Herod was insecure because he was a man of pride committed to the world of the flesh and the devil. He knew that John the Baptist was innocent, but he let John the Baptist die because of pride. He let John the Baptist lose his head because, ironically, Herod did not want to lose face. In the seventeenth century in England, King Charles II was given evidence that St. Oliver Plunkett, whom he had sentenced to death, was innocent. And Charles himself, who died a Catholic, recognized the injustice of the sentence that had been passed. But he also knew, accord-ing to the code—the royal protocol—that he could not rescind that judgment without greatly endangering himself politically. So he let the burden of guilt be placed upon those who had perjured themselves, and Plunkett became a martyr.

In our day, the Supreme Court, in a review of the *Roe v. Wade* decision on abortion, its 1992 *Casey* decision, and many since, basically said that we recognize that the abortion decision was wrong and unjust, but we really cannot revise it now, for we might lose face. Our whole system of jurisprudence might be mocked and be called into doubt. In the spiritual struggle, God gives us power to fight, but we have to have authority as well to use the power that authority confers in the right way, or else we let all kinds of injustice and death into the world. As recounted in the Gospel according to St. Luke, Our Lord gives power and authority to His disciples to cast out evil spirits (9:1).

Only with God's permission—God, Who is the source of all authority and concomitant power in human history—can we order power God's way and win His great battle.

Pontius Pilate said to Our Lord, "Do you not know that I have power to release you, and power to crucify you?" Our Lord said, "You would have no power over me unless it had been given you from above" (John 19:10–11). Yes, Pilate had power, but he had no authority. And then the Scriptures said something very strange. Pilate announces that Jesus is innocent and therefore He will have Him scourged.

It is a strange line. He will scourge Him, though innocent, because Pilate does not want to lose face, facing the people. That is the same stupidity we commit every day when we engage in merely human battle, without reference to the supernatural battle between God and Satan for the human soul.

On the Cross, Our Lord says, "Father, forgive them," and the sword pierces the heart of Our Lady at those very words. A sword! And we know what that sword is. It is that sword of justice that bursts into flame at the gates of Eden. Our Lord's heart is pierced on the Cross by a soldier's lance, but it really is the sword of justice opening His heart that we might see the divine love. That same sword pierces Our Lady's heart in that same moment, and when their two hearts are opened, we see a sight that was denied to Adam and Eve. And that sight is Paradise itself.

Casting Out Fear with Perfect Love

To consider Our Lord frightening is not irreverent. He Himself said many times, "Do not be afraid," in recognition of the fear He could engender, especially when He performed signs and wonders. After the Resurrection, He counseled His Apostles, "Fear not," knowing how frightened they must have been to witness Him risen from the dead. And yet Our Lord also counseled that "the fear of the LORD is the beginning of wisdom" (Prov. 9:10). It is no contradiction. After all, there are two kinds of fear, even as there are two kinds of life.

The first kind of fear is physical. We are physical beings, and our physical life begins at conception. We become afraid when our assumptions about the physical order seem to be contradicted, when unexpected things occur in the physical order of things. But we also live spiritually. Our moral being becomes alive when we become not merely some*thing*, which happens at conception, but when we become some*one*. This does not in any way deny the physical, legal fact of personhood, which is proclaimed at the moment of conception and must be safeguarded at all costs by society from the moment of conception. But, morally, we become alive to the world and to the world's God when we recognize that we are more than some*thing*, that we are some*one* appointed by God to be with Him forever and, at the beginning of this journey, to serve Him on earth.

As physical fear is part of our physical life, so is this other kind of fear—spiritual fear or holy fear—part and parcel of our moral awakening. It is this holy fear that God means when He says that "the fear of the LORD is the beginning of wisdom." That holy fear is something that we experience only when we have become spiritually some*one*. The tyrant who keeps cropping up in history wants us to be some*thing*—not some*one*. It is this malignant figure who constantly addresses people as though they are just things. They address mobs, they speak of masses, they speak of the people's government, the people's paradise, but there is no individual. The individual is lost in the crowd, and only the crowd counts.

This tyranny over the soul is totally transformed by Our Lord, for He is the Lord of life. He gives us a name. He gives us a moral identity. And He shows us the glory of being someone through the examples of the saints. Pope Leo the Great said, "Man, remember your dignity." That remembrance requires an act of the will in a world that wants us to forget our humanity, our human dignity. Are we to be merely somethings, or are we to be someones?

On the Cross, our Lord hung between two thieves. One we call the bad one and the other the good one. They probably were not actually thieves at all, but insurrectionists. And the one we call the bad one had a problem: he thought of himself as only a thing. He was part of the human psychology, which is easily seduced, more often than not, in the early years of life by lust, and in the middle years by power, and in the waning years of life by avarice. He was probably in the second stage. We assume that these delusions are always going to lead to our downfall. But they might not.

There is lust as a consequence of the flesh, but we see how Cleopatra and Joan of Arc, two women of beauty, followed divergent paths in using their beauty. We may assume that the quest for wealth will always dissolve the integrity of the soul, and so it did with Nero, who built himself a golden house in Rome. But there was also Katharine Drexel of Philadelphia, who inherited the equivalent in contemporary terms of some billion dollars and used it for the spread of the gospel.

Power need not reduce us to mere things. It did that, possibly, to Napoleon. But the right uses of power raised King Louis IX, of that same nation of France, to the altars of the Church. This bad thief was condemned to victimhood, all because he saw himself as only a thing; he did not understand that there could be a moment when he could become someone and that, in that moment, lust could become love, power could become holy zeal, and avarice could become a hunger for the treasury of the saints.

Three hundred years before the Resurrection, after the Peloponnesian War, the Greek Thucydides wrote describing the decline of the world's culture around him. After listing the moral rot, he uttered a sigh and said rather cynically, "What more can you expect of human nature?" About three hundred years after the Resurrection, a saint, Basil the Great, wrote describing the collapse of Roman imperial civilization, and it sounds very much like the moral collapse that so agitated Thucydides. But, instead of sighing cynically, Basil became righteously indignant and said, "Christians, how can you allow this to happen to yourselves? Do you not realize that you have been bought at a great price?" That's the difference that the Resurrection makes.

The Resurrection spreads fear in the world among people who think of themselves only as things because they know that the human thing is not supposed to rise from the dead. But Our Lord says, "Be not afraid. I am not a ghost, for a ghost does not have flesh and bones as you see that I have. Recognize Who I am; be not faithless but believing" (see Luke 24:39; John 20:27). That is the voice of Our Lord to things, summoning them to be people. If we are only things, we are going to think in a two-dimensional way, without that third spiritual dimension—that wealth condemns us to avarice; that intelligence condemns us to a life of skepticism; that if we are poor, we must always be resentful; that if we are beautiful, we must be vain. Yet there have been many saints who were wealthy, intelligent, direly poor, and very beautiful. But they were not condemned by those gifts. Something happened to them! They recognized that they were more than things. They did not suffer the presumed fate of that poor man hanging on the one side of Our Lord.

How did they avoid being taken in by these temptations—seeing themselves only biologically? There are five ways the Church traditionally offers, and those saints took them to heart. One is the gift of natural law—observing the world the way God wants us to observe it, through His holy law written in the heart, the conscience. There is also the gift of the Ten Commandments. There is also the voice of Christ speaking in history. There is the voice of Christ speaking specifically through His Church in Her doctrines. And, finally, there is what St. Paul calls, in his letter to the Romans, the fifteenth chapter, "spiritual obedience to reality." He says that he has gone all over the world as he knew it, from Jerusalem to Alericum, using words and deeds, offering his own example, and finally giving the Holy Spirit to the people to lead them into holy obedience. The Holy Spirit is the One who ultimately opens our eyes to the supernatural consciousness of the human mystery.

The physical world will not be frightened if we obey the Holy Spirit. The tyrant has always been insecure. He is living merely on the physical level, and he has persuaded all his subjects for so long that they are mere things that he begins to suspect that he may be nothing more than a thing himself. Tyrants boast of their greatness. They have always done that through history. They have built monuments to their greatness really out of a quiet hysteria, a suspicion that they were not that great at all. Herod liked to be called "the Great," and he is famous, amongst other things in architecture, for the large stone blocks that he used for building construction. The stones he used had to be larger than the stones that others used—a sign of insecurity as well as grandeur.

What really constitutes greatness? Louis XIV, it turned out in his autopsy, had a stomach five times the normal size. But the size of his stomach did not make him great. Catherine of Russia was called "the Great," but she treated men like horses. Tiberius, the Roman emperor at the time of the Crucifixion, was the most powerful man in the world, and he was able to command anything within human possibility. He asked for the most perfect mirror in the world. He had grown tired of the rough mirrors normally available. We get an indication of that when St. Paul says we look now through a glass darkly (1 Cor. 13:12).

Tiberius had a competition for a perfect mirror, and one close to perfection was produced. It may have been the first use of mercury in a mirror. Whether this is so is unknown, but what is known is that he was satisfied with his reflection in it. And he had the inventor summoned into his presence, thanked him, and then had him executed. Tiberius could not risk having that inventor produce a second mirror because someone else in the world might have a mirror as fine as his. That is insecurity writ large.

Similarly, the story is told of Ivan the Terrible, who had the Cathedral of St. Basil built in Moscow. Two architects worked on it and when they finished, Ivan was very pleased to possess what he thought to be the most beautiful building in the world. He had the two architects brought into his presence and asked if they could produce another building like this. "Yes, Sire," they replied, and so he had their eyes gouged out.

All these tyrants were afraid with an unholy fear. They thought the whole world was nothing but things, and they themselves were things amongst all the others. Bishop François Fénelon of France, who wrote the *Adventures of Telemachus* at the turn of the seventeenth century, said in a sermon, "My brothers, what are you afraid of? What are you afraid of—of leaving that which is going to someday leave you anyway? What are you afraid of—of finding too much goodness? What are you afraid of—of loving too much? What are you afraid of?" And what are we afraid of? St. John in his first letter, says, "Perfect love casts out fear" (4:18).

This is the John who stood at the foot of the Cross—a living example of his words. It was a frightening thing to see someone crucified, and he was a young innocent fellow who probably had not seen anything so horrible. The other Apostles, older than he, had fled. Do you not think he wanted to do the same? And yet next to him was Our Lord's Mother, the perfection of human love—not something but someone! She had all her life kept saying to herself, "People are calling me a thing, but I am someone. I remember once an angel told me that." And John stood by that Perfect Love, looking up at the Source of All Love, and so when he writes to the Churches, that is precisely what he says, "Perfect love casts out fear." He was not afraid at the foot of the Cross, and probably for the rest of his life he marveled about that himself. Our Lady looked up at the Cross and saw Her Son, and as she looked, she probably remembered when she was afraid for Him—when she and Joseph fled with the Child to Egypt. It was a long walk. They had spent much of their lives walking.

The Holy Family probably went to Jerusalem three times a year, 80 miles each way. That is 480 miles just on pilgrimage every year, on foot. It is said that the average person today walks 8,000 to 10,000 steps per day, and during the course of a lifetime, about 115,000 miles. We are meant to walk. Our feet are machines for walking—very extraordinary machines, complicated machines. We have twenty-six bones in each foot. Those fifty-two bones of our feet are about a quarter of all the bones in the human body. There are thirty-three joints in the foot, some hundred ligaments, tendons, and muscles. God wants us to walk. And, sometimes we have to walk very fast, and sometimes we have to flee.

Our Lady looked at our Lord's feet and remembered the times He fled. Remember, He fled from Nazareth when they were going to cast Him off the brow of the hill. But He was not afraid in an unholy way. As there is an unholy fear, so there is a holy fear and that holy fear is born of perfect love. The more we love, the more we will enter into the good kind of fear, and that is a fear of sin itself—sin and all the destruction it brings into the world.

St. Paul knew about that kind of fear, and after he had been changed by love from unholy fear to holy fear, he wrote to Titus:

> We know ourselves very well, very well indeed. There was a time when we were given to all those things, when we were given to incredulity and error when we were slaves to diverse desires. When we were hateful and hated others. But a change has come about now. We did those things because we were afraid. We thought we were something, and we thought we tried to be more than what we are, and we were disappointed. But when we met Perfect Love, all that fear was cast out, and with it sin. And there came into our hearts a holy fear that fears nothing that the world can put before us except the consequences of sin.

That is really the difference between the thief on the cross we call the bad one and the one we call the good. Our Lord said that there is only one Who is good, and that is God. But we call the one thief "good" because he was willing to let God come into his heart. He did not understand theology. He did not understand the identity of the One in the middle. But he understood very well that He was not afraid—that the Man in the middle was something more than a thing; and whenever he looked at the Man in the middle, he felt like someone and not just a thing. He knew that the Someone in the middle would be able to do with him what wealth or the quest for power or lust had not been able to do. And so this other thief cried out, "Jesus, remember me when You come into Your kingdom." He was not afraid to say that. He is the only one we have in the Gospel who called out His name — not a title: Rabbi, Master, or Lord. He simply said "Jesus."

In that very moment, perfect love had entered his heart and all fear of an unholy nature was cast out. That thief heard a voice saying to him, "Truly, I say to you, today you will be with me in Paradise" (Luke 23:43). In all of Jerusalem, trembling with fear of one thing or another, fear of the Romans, fear of the Supreme Court, fear of the priests, fear of themselves, there was one place where there was no fear, and it was on the hill of the Crucifixion. Perhaps there was one tremor, and it was from the other side of the Cross, from the one we call the bad thief. Our Lord, Who wants none of us to fear, wants us to realize that there is no need for any one of us ever to go down in history as bad. At the foot of the Cross, Our Lady was given to the Church to remind us of that sublime truth. Her prayers for us cast out fear. And we might invoke her prayer now on behalf of that other thief, the one we call bad, for prayers are retroactive; they live in eternity. And we might ask her to pray right now for that man, that in the last moments that he breathed, he, too, might have been willing, as an act of fearlessness, to call upon Our Lord by name. And, in so doing, we ask for prayer for ourselves as well.

Hail Mary, full of grace, the Lord is with Thee. Blessed art Thou among women, and blessed is the fruit of Thy womb, Jesus. Holy Mary, Mother of God, pray for us sinners now and at the hour of our death. Amen.

Living Will

The term "living will" is often misunderstood and abused. A living will, in the best sense of the term, is a generous offering of one's body for the good of others. When we die, our body can be used to help others through organ donation and the like. Of course, given today's medical advances, a living person can donate a kidney or bone marrow. It might be said laconically that there are some who do give the impression of being brain donors.

But a living will can have an entirely different meaning—something that is a contradiction of life. That is when it is not offered in a spirit of generosity but as a substitute for God's will—where an individual says he wants to decide when he wants to die, apart from tributes to human dignity. He simply looks on life as a matter of existence, to be prolonged as long as comfortably possible and then to be annihilated. That, of course, is not a living, but a deadly, will. The figure a few decades back in our culture nicknamed "Dr. Death," who promoted what was euphemistically called "euthanasia," was promoting that kind of death. I remember that, to raise money for his legal expenses, there was an exhibition of some of his amateur paintings, many in lurid colors, showing the devil. The face of death always reveals itself.

Christ, too, had a living will. He Himself said that He had come into the world to do the will of His Father. He lived that will all His life. That was the "living will" for Him—from the very beginning of His earthly life. Our Lord was always aware of Who He was, and if people doubt that, they are simply betraying the fact that they are not quite sure who they themselves are. To wit, "God does not know Who He is. How could we possibly know who we are?" In fact, Our Lord in His divine nature always knew His Father was in Heaven. He had a human nature, which did not contradict His divine nature but was the vehicle by which His divine nature moved and breathed in His own creation. And that human nature had to be trained. It had to learn how to walk and to talk. Our Lady and St. Joseph taught Him those things. But when He was only twelve years old, in the Temple, He said to Mary and to Joseph, "How is it that you sought me? Did you not know that I must be in my Father's house?" (Luke 2:49).

When we picture that scene, we must remember what that Temple was. It was a combination of a cathedral and a train station and a slaughterhouse on a hot day, with all the sounds and stenches of those places. It was running with blood and the screams of animals and the stench of death, mingled with the sights of golden candelabra and silken vestments and the music of trumpets and the fragrance of incense. It was not your typical suburban church. This was His Father's house. And what did He mean? Our Lady did not ask Him. She simply kept these things in her heart.

The Temple is the house of the Father, and we go to the Temple to learn the Father's will. If we are filled with our own will, we will try to make the Temple into our own house. We will try to domesticate God. And the less the Holy Church in Her earthly manifestation understands Her supernatural identity, the more She will become bureaucratic in the worst sense. She will try to substitute Her own furniture for the furniture of divinity. I am talking about bureaucracies, committees, offices, buildings—some of which are necessary, though not as necessary as they might seem.

Bureaucracy can be like an eating disorder, and the more depressed one is, the more one eats. And the more a Christian is unaware of his glory and the mystery of the Church, the more he may go to meetings and establish commissions and get busy doing "churchy" things—all as a sign that he has forgotten that this is really the house of the Father. Alexis de Tocqueville, the French visitor to our country in the early days of our Republic, said, and I'm paraphrasing, "The problem with bureaucracy is that it bends, softens and weakens the will. It does not destroy things so much as it prevents things from being born." There was a lot of that in Jerusalem two thousand years ago. There were officials who thought that the Temple was their house and their house alone. They spoke pious language, but they practiced as though it was only their house, and so they brought death into the world, and that is why Christ, even at age twelve, began the cleansing of that Temple with His speech, to the astonishment of the rabbis. Where did He get this ability to speak with such authority? Our Lady did not ask. She simply pondered these things in her heart.

Pope St. John Paul II said that we have to open the doors once again to Christ. We have to let Christ's living will back into the world. And as He does the will of the Father, so we must do the will of the Son. In the Vatican Gardens, where this sainted Pope John Paul II would walk on nice days, saying his Breviary, there is a piece of the Berlin Wall. It was a gift to the Holy Father from the German people in thanksgiving for the role he played in the conquest of the atheistic tyranny that strangled eastern Germany and much of the world. That wall came tumbling down even as the walls of Jericho came tumbling down, because we can resist the divine will only for so long. Inevitably our stubbornness comes crashing down on us, just like the Berlin Wall.

Our Lady in the Temple, in the precincts where the women could stand, looked at her twelve-year-old Boy and must have thought to

herself almost exactly what Louise Soubirous, mother of St. Bernadette, thought in the nineteenth century when her daughter claimed
to be having conversations with the Blessed Mother. Louise went
with the other women of Lourdes to see for herself what was going
on. She was distressed and fearful that her daughter might be losing
her mind. And as she watched Bernadette in the Grotto looking up
at what Louise could not see and moving her lips with words Louise
could not understand, she said, "That is not my daughter." Our Lady
might have been tempted to say the same thing. But she did not.
One of the only things Our Lady ever said, at least as recorded in
the Gospels, was "Let it be done to me according to Your word."
She was speaking to God. Whatever thoughts passed through her
mind, she was immaculately in harmony with the will of God.

Little children may think they "know it all" simply because
they do not realize how much there is to know. A six-year-old boy
said of his big brother, "I have been putting up with him all my
life!" And for a six-year-old, that may seem a great burden; yet
it is only six years. But when Our Lord was thirty years old, He
went out into the world burdened with all eternity, for while He
was thirty years old on earth at the beginning of His ministry, He
was also the I AM, the Beginning and the End in the flesh. And
what was His Father's will? It was spelled out on the Cross. In his
divine nature, Jesus Christ knew He must die for the salvation of
the world. His human nature had to be instructed from childhood
in how humans die. When He was a small boy, He might very well
have seen strange shapes on the horizon. Going over the brow
of a hill, it is very possible He saw one of those massive Roman
executions of the day, when hundreds were crucified. Then, there
was at least one occasion, in His boyhood, when some four to five
thousand insurrectionists were crucified. This little Boy wandered
out onto the roads and could see these strange machines shaped
like the Greek letter tau, and, as He got closer, He could see dead

men on them with their bones through their flesh and their eyes pecked out by birds of prey, their lower limbs gnawed at by wild dogs. And possibly, Joseph came down the path to pull Him away from such a horrific sight. The little Boy kept looking back. All the while, Mary pondered these things in her heart.

Our Lady began to find what Christ was about when she lost Him in the Temple. For three days, she and Joseph sought Him, sorrowing. And that is always the case. The finding of Christ involves a loss to begin with. If we have become accustomed to the virtue of faith, we really find the depth of faith. When we have gone through those minutes in which it seems we have been losing our faith, if we are accustomed to being of a rather cheerful and optimistic nature, we only really begin to understand the virtue of genuine hope as a gift from heaven in those moments when we have, as the world says, hoped against hope. And it is only when love seems betrayed, when we have been disappointed by those we have loved and thought loved us, that we begin to understand why love is mixed up with the Man on the Cross.

Losing and finding are two inexorably linked sides of the same coin of religion. And thank God, literally, that we go through losses. Without those losses, we would never discern the will of God. By contrast, superficial religion consists in trying to see the dawn without having traveled through the darkness. Superficial worship consists of trying to be in communion with God without making a sacrifice. It has happened across our culture, even at the holiest moment of the Mass, where congregants believe they are at a benign, congenial gathering without recognizing that there looms over the altar the Crucified One, victorious in our lives only because of His awful death for us. Superficial religion wants the consolations of religion without moral obedience. Christ saves us from all that by letting us, from time to time, think we have lost Him. St. John Chrysostom said that, and I am paraphrasing, "When

A Crisis in Culture

Our Lord said to His Mother, 'Why did You seek Me, sorrowing?' He was not increasing Her perplexity. He was speaking to Her that way so as to free her from any danger of tyrannical affection so that she might enter more deeply into the mystery of who He was and, therefore, by so doing, she might become the Servant, ever more faithfully, of God, recognizing that Her Son was her own Master." And when that happened, then she could become *Salus Infirmorum*, "Health of the Sick"; *Refugium Peccatorum*, "Refuge of Sinners"; *Consolatrix Afflictorum*, "Consolation of the Afflicted"; *Auxilium Christianorum*, "Help of Christians." Our Lady, immaculately, in her humility followed the will of God even when she did not understand it. And so she was free of legalism — that kind of grim enduring of God's law rather than embracing it.

Legalism is a begrudging service of God. God is a generous giver, and we cannot receive His graces if we serve Him in such a begrudging, legalistic way. The story is told of a woman who told her four-year-old daughter to take care of her baby brother for a short space of time while she was out of the house. When she returned, having told the little girl that under no circumstances was she to pick up her brother, she found both children missing. Panic-stricken, the mother hurriedly ran from room to room in the house and finally found her children in an upstairs room playing blithely on the floor. Relieved, yet annoyed, she said, "I told you never to pick up your brother." And the girl said, "I didn't," prompting her mother to ask, "Well, how did he get here?" The little girl pertly replied, "I rolled him all the way."

That was the crime of the Pharisees, of the legalists whom Our Lord put up with day in and day out during His earthly ministry. But Our Lady did not look for loopholes in the divine will. She abandoned herself to it.

Our culture is in crisis now because it has thwarted the divine will. It is angry at nature because it does not understand nature as a manifestation of the divine will, which is why our culture has tried to contradict nature. It has brought a culture of death into the world by persuading lawyers that they are supposed to find ways around justice rather than champion justice. They have persuaded physicians, in some instances, that they are to bring death, not healing, into the world. They have even persuaded women that they should not allow life to come through them and that they should be angry at their womanhood even as men have been persuaded that they should be angry at their manhood.

It is an old story that goes back to the beginning of the human race. But even the pagan Greeks understood it. They lived it, and they explained it quite eloquently, as did Euripides, the dramatist, during his final years in Macedonia in the Court of Archelaus I. In his play *The Bacchae*, he describes a situation in Thebes. An old man named Cadmus has a daughter, Agave. Her son is the young king Pentheus. Agave has decided that she is no longer going to worship the local gods. Instead, she is going to go out after the god of revelry. For, by worshipping him, nature can be turned upside-down and women can be like men. And so she and her lady friends go into the forest, and they dance and they drink themselves into a stupor, waving spears, proclaiming themselves hunters as strong as men. Her son Pentheus furtively goes to the edge of the wood, climbs a tree, and watches this unseemly orgy—the women behaving with each other as they should with men, dressed as men. Suddenly, Agave cries out that there is a lion in the tree. And the women go and pull the lion down and slay it with their fingernails to show that women are even stronger than men. They do not even need spears to do the deed. And they cut off the lion's head, and Agave goes back into the town holding the head with its golden mane. Agave confronts her father with her trophy, and old Cadmus realizes what she is really holding, and tells her to look to the sun. The sun sobers her enough to see that in her hand, held by his golden hair, is the head of her own son.

A Crisis in Culture

That was a play to the pagan Greeks. But it is a fact to our society at the present time. By our thwarting the divine will, death has come into the world. We have propagated death through injustice, through contempt for the poor, through a sense of despair about the mystery of death, a fear of what will happen to us in old age. Yes, even mothers have been persuaded to kill their own children in their own wombs. It is not the will of Our Father in Heaven that we should be motherless on earth. This is why, when we call upon such noble women as St. Elizabeth Ann Seton or St. Frances Cabrini, we instinctively call them "Mother." It is the voice of a motherless society that is learning again, through a loss of motherhood, what a great gift motherhood is. Elizabeth Seton lived a domestic life of bliss in her early years in old New York. Hers was a rather prosperous family of social distinction, and things seemed to be going her way. But then her husband went bankrupt, and she found herself with him across the ocean, holding his hand as he died, and her whole world seemed to fall apart. But it was in that loss that she began to find the fullness of Christ's revelation in His Holy Church, and she is now known to us as St. Elizabeth Ann Seton. But we call her Mother Seton because she and women like her have learned through loss, through suffering, through failures, how great a treasure God has given us in His Son. Elizabeth Ann Seton found Christ most vividly in the Blessed Sacrament of the altar.

We might call Our Heavenly Mother, the Virgin Mary, the sacrament of the divine will, for she, while not divine, did the will of God, who is divine. We only have to look to her to see what that will is. Francis Thompson wrote:

> Does the fish soar to find the ocean,
> The eagle plunge to find the air —
> That we ask of the stars in motion
> If they have rumor of thee there?

Nor need we to look to heaven to see the divine will. We need only look into the Immaculate Heart of Our Lady, manifest at the foot of the Cross, not asking why or how all this should be but simply remembering that Her Son is doing the will of His Father.

In the twenty-fifth chapter of the Gospel according to St. Matthew, Our Lord says that the Master will someday say, "Depart from me, you cursed, into the eternal fire prepared for the devil and his angels; for I was hungry and you gave me no food, I was thirsty and you gave me no drink, I was a stranger and you did not welcome me, naked and you did not clothe me, sick and in prison and you did not visit me" (vv. 41–43). But there's one thing the Master will never say to us. He will never say, "Depart from Me because you loved My Mother too much." His Mother is His living will to you and to me.

Behold the Man

You may be familiar with these exotic names: Ahab, Jezebel, Jehoshaphat. About nine hundred years before the birth of Our Lord, Ahab was misruling the kingdom of Israel, and his wife, Jezebel, was accompanying him in misrule — so vividly that few girls are named after her today, lest they emulate their namesake. In the kingdom of Judah, King Jehoshaphat was struggling to wipe out idolatry.

As all that was going on, across the Mediterranean, in the culture of the Greeks, blind Homer, the poet, was singing his lines about man wandering around the world — a pre-jet-era "world" that was essentially limited to the Mediterranean basin. It was the world that mattered to Homer and his tribes, as reflected in *The Odyssey*, in which Homer describes man wandering, trying to get back home again. It is the history of the human adventure. He sings that line, in Greek, "Sing to me, O muse, of man and all his ways."

Man does not have one way. He has many ways. That's why he gets lost. He is a very complicated thing — which is how we get poetry and philosophy. If we analyze human complexity with the eyes of the poet, or the eyes of the philosopher, we will be amazed — and also confused. The only way we can see the complexity of man — not as a maze in which we get lost, but as a shadow of eternal glory — is to look at the essential man.

A Crisis in Culture

Two thousand years ago in Jerusalem, Pontius Pilate said, "Behold the Man" (John 19:5, Douay Rheims). But, the crowd at the foot of the balcony did not want to look. That crowd was, of course, an abstraction; the term "crowd" is a figure of speech. You cannot address crowds. The individuals in the crowd are the real reality; a crowd is a collection of people, each part of the human adventure in all their myriad ways. Each one of us knows about the self and how confusing we are. And we do not want to behold the one Man Who is not confused. So the crowd, that collection of individuals, shifts its eyes to Pontius Pilate, whom they can more easily understand because he is like them. And it's no use simply pointing to those people in the crowd, or to Pontius Pilate, because they are just like us. The crowd can understand the psychology of Pilate. He is like them. He can be stroked, cajoled, bribed, flattered. He is weak too. They know it because they themselves are weak.

We can instinctively spot in others our own flaws. Pilate was conspicuously weak — so conspicuously weak that he kept talking about how strong he was. "Do You not know that I have power over You?" he said to Christ. He was insecure. We know that because he sat on a marble throne, and he made sure there was a golden figure of an eagle flying behind him. And so the crowd says, "If you let this Man go, we know you are no friend of Caesar" (see John 19:12). "Friend of Caesar" was a technical title, and it was a political license to let Pilate exercise certain privileges. And because he was weak and insecure, he could not risk losing that title, and so he let Jesus go — not back to Nazareth but to the Cross. "The Man" goes to His death. And along the way, His barefoot feet are cut and He stumbles, for the first time. And the people are embarrassed. Then He stumbles a second time, and the people are more embarrassed. The third time He stumbles, the wailing of the women is heard throughout the city, and they do not want to look at "the Man."

And what does He stumble over? If there had been a big rock in front of Him, the soldiers would have led Him around it. His wounded feet stumble over little stones, for He is "the Man," and, in His perfection, He feels all imperfection. We should remember that when we say the sin that we committed yesterday was not a big sin, not a mortal sin—just a venial sin. "Behold the Man," and see that there is no such thing as a little sin. I do not mean that in a scrupulous way or a compulsive way or a neurotic way. God in His mercy lets us know that there are different kinds of sins, and some can be sins unto death, and some can threaten us in other ways. But if we keep looking at "the Man," we will never underestimate the seriousness of any flaw in our complicated wonder.

Our Lord shows us through the confusing maze of history by offering each one of us a cross. That is how we enter into His journey through culture. The aforementioned Bishop François Fénelon said, "Refusing to accept your cross for any reason whatsoever is not to free yourself of a burden. It is to impose upon yourself an even heavier cross." The heaviest cross is not to have a cross. That is the double-cross of life, for it deprives us of association with "the Man." We follow Christ along the path through history by taking up the cross. All great civilizations have become great because people have been willing to shoulder burdens—not begrudgingly but joyfully, because they had some understanding of what man and his cross are. They have not always gotten it right, but they have produced great art, and they have built great buildings, and they have invented wonders because they have known that there is a splendor about the human condition.

Lieutenant General Sir Adrian Paul Ghislain Carton de Wiart VC, KBE, CB, CMG, DSO, in the British Army was seriously wounded in the Second World War. While recovering in Ireland, he was charmed when he asked a girl in County Mayo which way this country path led and she replied, "Sir, this path will take you wherever you want to go."

A Crisis in Culture

That is the voice of "the Man" to each one of us as we look at our culture and seem dismayed at the roadmap.

I live in Midtown Manhattan, right now near Penn Station. Earlier in my Manhattan sojourn, I lived right by Grand Central Terminal. And if you dropped dead on the east side of the information booth, I was the one who would go and give you last rites. An astonishing thing about that terminal is that while I have passed through it what seems like ten thousand times, I always seem to come out a different way. How many billions of people are in our world—each one with his own entrance into this culture, and his own exit.

To the pagan, it all seems confusing, but to the Christian, it is all part of a divine plan. That is why Scripture says that the Lamb of God was sacrificed from the foundation of the world (see Rev. 13:8, Douay-Rheims). The pagan will ask, "Why do bad things happen to good people?" You cannot look at "the Man" and say we are good. He Himself says that: " No one is good but God alone" (Mark 10:18). The question we should ask instead when we take up the cross is, "Why do good things happen to bad people?" We are blemished, but why does God allow us to walk with Him through history?

Take up the cross and realize there is no such thing as bad Friday. It's Good Friday. Every tragedy that we walk through with Christ becomes a blessing. The church where I lived in New York burned to the ground a few years ago, and everyone agreed that it was a tragedy. There are a number of places that would, surely, be better candidates for accidentally being burned to the ground—for the city's good. Why this church? The first Good Friday after that fire, we moved services to the ballroom of the Roosevelt Hotel, which, by coincidence, is the very room in which, during the stockholders' meeting scene in the film *Wall Street*, the leading character, played by Michael Douglas, uttered his now famous line: "Greed is good." It was because of the fire that the truth of Christ was preached on that same spot. The next year, services were held in the Waldorf-Astoria hotel, and people came to hear the Passion who would have never darkened—or shall we say brightened—the door of any church, and we had several confessionals, with confessions heard for five or six hours. If the church building had not burned, all those absolutions would never have been uttered, in that famous hotel, of all places.

Our Lord has seen all our suffering and all our tragedy. "The Man" has always been there. He was with the Greeks as they fought the battle of Thermopylae, and in our own century, He has been there during all the shedding of blood across the continents. He was there at that worst of all battles, at Verdun, the longest of the First World War, when hundreds of thousands of men were mowed down by new "machine guns," their own generals failing to anticipate the horror that these new inventions were unleashing in the world. It was very moving to say Mass on that spot where so much blood had been shed and to offer the blood of "the Man" for those who had died. People are not abstractions, and their deaths are not abstractions. Our Lord has been with us through all our crises, all through history, from the foundation of the world, and that is why, in His agony, He sweat blood. He was a human wine-press—the wine turned to blood. His suffering was Eucharistic. In 1586 in England, the daughter of the sheriff of York, Margaret Clitherow, died for the Holy Catholic Faith. She was pressed to death: a board was placed on her and heavy stones placed on top of the board. More than rocks weighed down upon Our Lord. Every sin ever committed or that ever will be committed, all the wars, pressed down on Him. And we say, "It shouldn't have happened to Him." But that's the giveaway. The minute we say it should not have happened, we are looking at "the Man."

St. Basil said, "The only reason we have a sense of justice, the only reason we say it should not have happened is because we have seen 'the Man.'" We know justice because justice has been revealed to us in the Perfect Man. Only the Christian can cry out fully in indignation against injustice, because the Christian has seen the full revelation of human dignity. The pagan does not object to injustice. He may speak of injustice, and he may speak of justice, but when justice fails, the pagan will shrug his shoulders and say, "Well, life is absurd anyway." Our culture is being seduced by that paganism. It has begun to think that suffering itself is absurd, that the offering of a cross is a curse. And that is why we hide from the truth. Anything unpleasant we can't understand, any evidence of the complexity of the human order, we tend to shy away from. We look for pop philosophers, gurus, self-help experts, and government assistance—even drugs—to hide the big problem. That is how we get euphemisms, which are nothing more than verbal fig leaves. Soldiers used to speak of "killing the enemy." Now they speak of "servicing the target." An airline spokesman announced the crash of a 727 by saying that the airplane had experienced a radical conversion. There are people in our society who say that a doctor who kills a baby in the womb is a health-care provider. We are wearing costumes passed on to us by our first ancestors—costumes woven to hide their shame. Lying about the mystery of the human order is the worst form of barbarism.

Pope Leo the Great, in A.D. 452, confronted Attila the Hun and told him to go away. And he did. Three years later, Pope Leo confronted Gaiseric, king of the Vandals. Though Leo was powerless to make this barbarian go away, at least he persuaded him not to destroy the whole city. Pope St. John Paul II and his successors have done the same thing in our culture. And, every Christian has the responsibility to do the same. And who is the barbarian? Not Attila or Gaiseric but rather a new barbarian—every smooth talker who wants us to think that we can live by euphemisms.

Christ is the High Priest Who intercedes between our broken world and His glorious kingdom. He is the High Priest, and by virtue of His priesthood we can all pray, and that is why we are a priestly people. And that is why He ordained certain men to offer in His name His own Body as a living sacrifice on behalf of the human order.

A priest who has written several novels often complained to journalists about how he disagreed with the Church's teachings on this and that, and in particular on the priesthood. Nevertheless, he said he continued to be a priest because he liked it. He liked the ethnic traditions of Catholicism. He liked the customs attached to Catholic living. He liked the sociological implications of being Catholic in the world. But if we really understood the priesthood, we would not like it, because at the heart of the priesthood is the Cross. Peter did not like his priesthood. He fled from it. But in an act of humility, he carried his own cross up the Janiculum Hill in Rome because he did something more than like his priesthood. We can like puppy dogs. We can like ice cream. We cannot like a cross. Peter loved the priesthood because he loved the Cross, and he loved the Cross because he loved "the Man" on the Cross.

St. Paul tells us that he has received from the Lord Himself the truth that when we receive the wine and the bread at the altar, breathed upon by the Holy Spirit, it is no longer what we took to the altar. These elements now become the Body and Blood of the Lord, and if we drink of the cup and if we eat of the bread unworthily, we are doing so to our own condemnation (1 Cor. 11:23–30). It is only through the Cross that we understand that deep mystery.

Napoleon Bonaparte sentimentally said that the day of his First Communion was the happiest day of his life—but what did he do in consequence?

We can try to commune with God without taking up the cross. But by so doing we double-cross ourselves and our culture.

Twenty-three percent of all Catholics in the United States, according to a survey, say that they discern the Body and Blood of

A Crisis in Culture

Our Lord in the Holy Mass. What does that mean? It means that 77 percent of all those that call themselves Catholics have not beheld "the Man."

In one year alone, 3 bishops, 101 priests, 45 religious brothers, 64 women religious, and 28 lay catechists were martyred for the Faith throughout the world. The year was 1994, but if we count up the martyrs every year since — not counting numerous other Christians who have taken up crosses in less visible ways — the numbers would be similarly eye-popping.

I have had the honor of assisting at the Holy Eucharist with the most eminent late Cardinal Ignatius Kung of China. He witnessed to the gospel of "the Man" in Shanghai, Suzhou, Nanking as he spent more than thirty years in prison. He offered the Holy Sacrifice meticulously and cleansed the patens and the chalice with deep and reverent care, lest one particle be lost. After the Mass, he sat, and parents brought their little children up to let him touch them. Each one of those little children, when the years go by, will look back and know that, at that moment, they beheld "the Man."

The great men and women who have crossed the stage of this century witnessing to Christ were not supermen or superwomen. They did not fly through the air. They often crawled, bearing crosses. They were not without temptation. Thomas à Kempis said that temptations do not show our weakness. They show what a man is made of. A boy asked the sculptor Canova upon the unveiling of a statue, "How did you know that man was in there?" How did God know that people were waiting to form cultures in Mesopotamia, in Egypt, in China, in the Slavic world, in Africa, in Latin America, in our country? How does He know all who have been and are about to come? He is "the Man," and He offers Himself to us in His own Sacrament. St. Paul says in the First Letter to the Corinthians that we eat and drink to our own condemnation if we do not look at Him in the Holy Species. He says that is why some are sick and dying. And that is why our culture is a culture of death. But in the midst of this death, our Holy Father, St. John Paul II, said, "Man, become what you are." And how do we do that? By listening to the only sermon that Pontius Pilate ever preached and the only one that was true in spite of himself. It was the sermon he preached when he said to you and to me, in a culture of death, "Behold the Man."

Sign Language

Every year, tourists come to New York to see the Rockefeller Center Christmas Tree Lighting. And, being tourists, they do the logical thing: they go down Fifth Avenue to try to get as close as possible to the ceremonial lighting. But I have lived in this city long enough to know that if you just go around the corner, and down Fiftieth Street, nobody will be there, and you can walk right up to the tree and touch it. And I did! I mean, I have lived in Manhattan for so long that I finally thought I should do what the tourists do each Christmas and see my own tree.

Our Lord did very much the same thing. We are all, in a certain sense, tourists in this world—His world, which He invites us into. He knows the floor plan better than we do. We are always looking around for the big celebrities, the great messiahs. And then Our Own Creator comes into His creation down the side street—Bethlehem, where He was born. Nobody expected it to happen quite that way in spite of its being the fulfillment of a prophecy. First of all, they had no idea he would be born in a cave. Secondly, they had no idea that this Messiah would be the Lord of the Universe. Our Lord comes into the world quietly. Mary and Joseph did an ordinary thing when they went to Bethlehem for the census. They were not going to Bethlehem to celebrate Christmas and see the lights. They were following the little laws of the day, just like every other person at the time. But Our Lord was working through those little laws.

Twenty years ago, our Church was preparing to celebrate and offer as a gift to the Lord of Eternity the end of this second millennium and the coming of a whole new time for salvation history. There were various ways we were preparing for it. But the pope, St. John Paul II, in talking about approaching this change, reminded us that the year 2000 was a symbolic year. We do not know the precise year that Our Lord actually slipped into the world. According to some estimates, it might have happened six years earlier. If that was the case, no one really paid much attention to it. But that makes it all the more authentic, for only the angels paid attention to the Incarnation.

As the new millennium was approaching, some scholar claimed, not uniquely, on the basis of what he called "the latest research," that the Blessed Virgin had other children after the birth of Our Lord. What could this research be unless he happened to encounter a two-thousand-year-old midwife? There is no such research. For Our Lord searches our own hearts and reminds us that He came into the world as a unique offering, and Our Lady was a unique offering to Him. And, yes, she has many other children, but not biological, not born of her womb, which was consecrated to her God. Rather, we are sons of God by adoption, by an act of the will, by a profession of faith in Our Lord, and following the humility of our Blessed Lady, ever virgin. The perpetual virginity of Our Lady is not extraordinary. It is the sacrament of ordinariness. She does not do anything so extraordinary as to produce great prophets and great saints to follow in the train of Our Lord by giving birth to them. She offers herself in her humility and, indeed, in her solitude, the mother of that one Child, so that we might all, in our ordinariness and in our weakness, call her by the same title that Christ Himself uses: Mother.

G. K. Chesterson wrote in the *Home Book of Verse*, volume 1 (1912), that "the Christ Child stood at Mary's knee, His hair was like a crown, and all the flowers looked up at Him, and all the stars looked down." It is an ordinary scene. When we were children, we stood at our mother's knee. The flowers were there, and the stars were there too. The difference was a small difference. To the ordinary eye, we looked down at the flowers, and we looked up at the stars. When Christ stood at His Mother's knee, the flowers looked up to Him, and the stars looked down. The scene was so ordinary you might have missed it, and almost everyone did, except the holy angels.

The Romans had a saying, *Age quod agis*, "Do what you are doing." It is in obedience to Our God in the ordinary things—concentrating on the task at hand, doing what we are doing—that we find the way He secretly signals to us His plan of salvation. The liar, the obfuscator, the prince of pride does not want us to persevere in ordinary things and do what we are doing. He wants to dazzle us with spectacles. He wants to distract us with all kinds of vain temptations and illusions. He wants to drug us morally and physically so that we do not serve God in ordinary times, because Our Lord is the Lord of the ordinary. That is why the prince of lies will whisper into the ear of the mother, "Why don't you become a nun," even as he's whispering into the ear of the nun, "Why don't you become a mother?" He is whispering into the ear of the priest, "Why don't you become a husband and father," as he is whispering into the ear of the husband and father, "Why don't you become a priest?" He is whispering into the ear of many people these days, "Why don't you become the pope? You can do a better job." At the same time, he is whispering into the ear of the pope, "Why don't you go back to your country?" But the one who is whispering is that restless spirit, that stunning and spectacular Lucifer, who is anything but ordinary. He refused to follow God's plan. It was too ordinary for him, and he wants us to follow him in his misery. But all through his temptations, that One Lady perseveres in doing the ordinary things. She walks day by day from that well in Nazareth, carrying water to the little house to give to her baby. As the years pass, she finds herself having done nothing spectacular in the eyes of the world, having said nothing at all quoted in Scripture after the first miracle at Cana, and standing at the foot of the Cross as Her Son says, "I thirst." If you go into an art museum and someone rushes in and slashes the canvas, you will cry out for the guards. But if you are the artist of that canvas, you will weep. Our Lady wept when Her Son thirsted, for she, year after year, had hauled water to bring to Him and satiate His thirst. That was her Son. She gave herself at the foot of the Cross in Her agony. She could not give water to Him. She gave herself in her ordinary obedience of just being there. But by being there, she slaked His thirst as no drug, no myrrh, no vinegar on a sponge could slake it. She gave herself, and so we give ourselves, and that is the key to sanctity.

There are two kinds of people in this world, and they have consistently appeared on the stage of history: those who give their own blood for others and those who shed the blood of others for themselves. The second kind of person thinks that people do not count. They want spectacles. They want pageants. They want what they call power, and they have contempt for what they call the ordinary people, "the little people."

I remember giving a speech in which I quoted Lincoln's Gettysburg Address. And, to my astonishment, afterward a very old man came up to me and told me that his father, who had lived to a ripe old age, as a boy had stood under the platform at Gettysburg and heard the address on November 19, 1863, the day Lincoln gave it. In my talk I had quoted Lincoln's words about "the government *of* the people, *by* the people, and *for* the people." The only reason the man had come up to me was to tell me that his father always corrected people when they said it that way. His father would always remark, "That's not the way Mr. Lincoln said it! He said 'of the *people*, by the *people*, for the *people*!" The marvel of our constitutional government and the glory of all culture is not the preposition. It's not the "of" or the "by" or the "for" of living. What counts is the *people*! All the people! There is no such thing as *ordinary people*.

I went to see the body of Lenin. He is still in the mausoleum in Red Square at Moscow. There is debate over what to do with the body. He had intended in his will to be buried next to his mother, but she is in consecrated ground, and there is reluctance to allow that man who had raised his fist against God to be buried in a holy grave. We used to have to wait three or four hours to go in and see his body. I just walked in. The ceremonial guards are gone. I got some cinder in my eye; the air was quite polluted. To my self-shame, I found tears rolling down my cheek as I went into that tomb. As I stood in front of the tomb with the tears rolling down, I had a suspicion that the one guard remaining was looking at me and wondering: Was he looking at the last Leninist in Moscow? Who was this mad priest? I tell you: Lenin was dead, very dead, extremely dead, terminally dead.

Across Red Square, there is a new church, and electric lights over the door announce, "Christ is risen." And on the wall of a building where Lenin's portrait used to hang is now a five-story-high icon of St. George slaying the dragon. Lenin never spoke the way Lincoln did. He was fascinated with the prepositions of life, with the mechanics of government, but not with the *people*. He spoke so much about the people that you knew that he was betraying a guilty disregard for them. Individuals were expendable because people counted only for what they could do for him. He would never shed his blood for them; they would shed their blood at his command, for him.

A Crisis in Culture

It is because ordinary people doing ordinary things find the glory of God in this ordinary world that God bids us to look upon our ordinariness and see how we fail in the little things of life in trying to serve Him. Those failures we call sins. Our sins are not going to destroy the world. We are, each one of us, quite unnecessary to the universe. But our sins can loom so large in our lives that they can make us think that we are all that counts. When that happens, we become contemptuous of the ordinary people God calls the saints. The real saints, therefore, are full of joy when they meet someone willing once again to listen to the ordinary voices through which God speaks. Dostoyevsky, in the novel *The Brothers Karamazov*, describes, through the voice of the young Alyosha, Father Zosima. Alyosha said the strange thing about Fr. Zosima is that he was always happy. He always seemed cheerful and, stranger than that, this holy man seemed particularly happy in the presence of sinners, when they called themselves sinners. He seemed to be more cheerful with them and more generous with them than with other people. And when he had forgiven them of their sins, he acted as though they had done him a favor. What was spectacular about Zosima was that he saw glory in weakness, in littleness. And that glory is manifested once the little confess themselves as little, the weak confess themselves as weak. St. Louis de Montfort said that the devil suffers more as the result of the humility of the Virgin Mary than he does when he is crushed by God. Such an extraordinary thing to say. But why does he suffer more in the presence of such humility? God is God! And it is of His very nature, His essence, to destroy the contradiction of God. But Mary had a choice. She had freedom. And, in her littleness, she manifested the glory of God by making her ordinary life available to Him. And the prince of pride could not stand that. God crushes him, yes, and he suffers greatly because of it. But he is absolutely humiliated when an ordinary human conquers him through the grace of God.

It is when we are humble that we begin to understand that God's words are more extraordinary than they seem at first reading. If we try to look for profundity, we only project our own pedantry when we read the Scriptures. People have looked, for instance, at the fifth chapter of St. Paul's Letter to the Ephesians and in the third chapter of his Letter to Colossians, where he talks about marital relations, where, among other things, he writes that a wife should obey her husband. People think they are being profound when they say, "Well, this is a culturalism—a kind of patriarchal prejudice, a chauvinism." And they have gone so far as to convince the world of that, that there are some people who even want to edit those words out of the Word of God. But if we are humble, we will understand that there is a majesty and a drama in those words that does not demean women or demean men, but lets us know what marriage and love and the divine romance of Christ the Bridegroom for His Church are all about. These are not ordinary words. They are not political words. Those letters form what look like ordinary words, but they are hymns of love being sung to the world by heaven. And it is only if we are humble enough that we will understand that God mystically is showing us how great we can be if we will only be humble and ordinary in His service.

That is why Our Lord thirsts for souls. He thirsts for us because He wants us. He has a plan for us. And if we try to figure out that plan in what we consider sophisticated ways, we are going to miss the majesty of the divine revelation that comes to us in the ordinary signs and symbols. I suppose the greatest sign of all, if we want to know how much God loves us, is His thirst on the Cross. I was waiting in the train station in Newark on one occasion for a friend to collect me when a group of youths entered the waiting room dressed in rather violent-looking attire—black leather jackets and chains and so on. And I thought this is a time for an Act of Contrition. Then I noticed that they began doing something very beautiful. They were dressed very horribly, but they were making very beautiful signs with their hands. They were using sign language. I had misjudged them. They were on a school outing from some academy for the deaf, and their deafness required them to do something more lovely with their hands than I could do. Our Lord, in His humility, took the form of a slave, and people turned away from Him. They misjudged Him. When He cried from the Cross and said, "I thirst," they thought they had the measure of the man — that He was simply dehydrating. Little did they know that He was, in that moment, turning that awful machine of the Cross into heavenly sign language.

The Cross is the sign that Our Lord wants us with Him. And what could be a more ordinary sign? There is nothing spectacular about two pieces of wood inelegantly put together in the most basic and obvious way. But if we have a humility that is willing to hear His voice through the Cross, we will understand what that sign of the Cross is saying. Our Lord thirsts for souls. An Italian Passionist priest, Blessed Dominic Barberi, in the early nineteenth century, thirsted for souls. He prayed that he might be able to travel from Italy to England so as to reconvert the formerly Catholic island nation back to the faith of its fathers. He was told that this was simply impossible. He was a very ordinary man, not a profound theologian, and he spoke no English, which was perhaps the most obvious obstacle to his mission. But by hook or crook, he was determined to make the journey and was finally permitted to sail for England. And after many vicissitudes, he received a message that there was a young scholar at the University of Oxford who wanted to see him. He went there, and, in 1845, he received John Henry Newman into the Church. That was just the beginning of a reconversion of a whole culture that is only now really beginning to make its mark on Christian life, accelerated with the canonization of St. John Henry Cardinal Newman on October 13, 2019 — which began only because that man, Blessed Dominic Barberi, was willing to offer his ordinariness for souls. And as he walked every day along the path of his mission, he had a little sign on him, and that was the sign of the Cross—that ordinary symbol that he took to perform true miracles.

The Holy Spirit breathes upon His Church, breathes upon Our Lady, and breathes upon all of the Apostles, who are very ordinary people, but they offer that ordinariness up to God and they see something marvelous happening. That ugly tool becomes the sign language of heaven and, as the flames descend upon them, I expect Our Lady is the first one ever to smile as she makes the Sign of the Cross.

The Grace of a Happy Death

A venerable prayer of the Church asks on behalf of the sick that they might have a speedy recovery or the grace of a happy death. It is not prayed much anymore. Possibly, there are people who think that, by mentioning death, we distract God from the request for recovery. But more problematic is the notion of a happy death. Our culture does not speak that way. It speaks rather tragically of a painless death, but not so readily of a happy death.

How can a death be happy? Sadness comes from a loss of a sense of purpose. And when death is only the finale, then it is a sad thing. A happy death is a death that is for a purpose. We know the purpose. In 1812, Charles-Maurice de Talleyrand-Périgord received news of the defeat of Napoleon at the Battle of Borodino, his Russian campaign, which he had opposed. Talleyrand had been a bishop of the Church and had renounced his office and, for all practical purposes, had renounced Christ, until he was on his deathbed. Then he sought a happy death. But when Talleyrand heard of this change in Napoleon's fortunes twenty-six years earlier, he had a more fatalistic attitude and said, "This is the beginning of the end." One hundred thirty years later, when news was received of the Battle of Egypt, and the Second World War, Winston Churchill said, "This is not the end. It's not even the beginning of the end, but it is the end of the beginning."

A Crisis in Culture

When God made the world, He looked upon what He had made and rested on the seventh day. That is what the Scripture says. And that is how we get Shabbat, the day of rest, the holy day. But something happened. Saturday was moved to Sunday. That is because Christ rose from the dead and showed us that the resting of God is not an abdication. It is not a conclusion or a finale. The holy day is the beginning of eternity. God never rests the way we rest. He looks and He sustains. When God looks upon His creation, then, by the very glance, He begins to guide the history of the life He had placed in this universe. God has a plan for our lives. Our being born is the beginning of that plan. Our death is part of the plan, but it is not the conclusion of the plan. On the Cross, Our Lords says, "It is finished" (see John 19:30). What he means is that it is accomplished. That portion of God's commission to Him has been fulfilled. But something else is going to happen. This is why He is the Messiah. He shows us the purpose of birth and of death. That is the content of Messiahship. The old idea of the Messiah was that He would be a political figure who would give us a longer peace on this earth. But the divine Messiah shows us eternal peace.

The self-styled Paper of Record in New York City, in one editorial several years ago, speaking of a man who specializes in putting sick people out of their misery—voluntary suicide, doctor-assisted suicide, as he euphemistically said—called him a messiah. And this newspaper referred to his "messianic crusade." Make that the messiah of futility—the macabre contradiction of the Divine Messiah. All he was able to offer in his misbegotten crusade was a substitute for a happy death, essentially a sad death, a conclusion, but not an event in an eternal process.

The saints, all through their lives, had little deaths. They are called mortifications. Mortification is a dying to self—a disciplining of our lower nature so that our lower nature will serve our higher nature, our spiritual vocation. The body is the temple of the Holy Spirit—not the Holy Spirit itself. Au contraire, it must be a servant. By mortifying the flesh, by disciplining our passions, we practice a daily dying to the self—all for a purpose. Because it is directed toward a purpose—our sanctification—it becomes "holy mortification." If it had no other purpose, mortification would simply be aestheticism at best, masochism at worst. As you watch some people jogging along the road, and you see people dieting, and in these exercise parlors, they do look as if they have gotten the whole concept of mortification wrong. Their mortifications only mortify others.

In the nineteenth century, the hymnographer Father Frederick William Faber, best known for "Faith of Our Fathers," wrote that, and I am paraphrasing, "When we look at the lives of the great ones, the holy saints, it may seem that we are looking at great mountains covered with snow, and we seem very small in comparison. But we must remember how mountains come into being. Those mountains are the result of cataclysms, of earthquakes, of great wrenching and suffering. Every saint is that kind of mountain. If we do not mortify ourselves in preparation for a happy death, all we can hope to do is to mortify others."

Alexander the Great conquered the whole known world by the age of thirty-three, the age of Our Lord on the Cross. It was his not infrequent practice to cut off the hands of the enemy so that no longer would they be able to take up arms against him. Our Lord does something quite different. He lets His own hands be offered for us, for He is not insecure. His authority is from heaven. And consequently, His death is far different from any other death. It is a death willed by heaven. Our Lord comes into the world to die. We come into the world to live. In the pagan world, death, at the very best, was the entrance into some kind of shadowy underground. And what was left was a certain tone of nostalgia.

A Crisis in Culture

The Greek poet Callimachus, upon hearing of his friend's death, wrote to him an ode that I think expresses very well the heroic Greek mood in the face of death.

> They told me, Hericlitus, they told me you were dead.
> They brought me bitter news to hear and bitter tears
>   to shed.
> I wept as I remember'd how often you and I
> Had tired the sun with talking and sent him down the sky.
> And now that thou are lying, my dear old Carian guest,
> A handful of grey ashes, long, long ago at rest.
> Still thy pleasant voices, thy nightingales, awake;
> For Death, he taketh all away, but them he cannot take.

For Callimachus, his friend had not come back and would not come back, but he heard the echo of his voice, the nightingale. That is nostalgia; we might say it is romance. But is it true? Are these voices alive outside the imagination? Go to Saint Petersburg in Russia and see the vast cemetery containing the bodies of the hundreds upon thousands — over six hundred thousand souls — who died during the siege of that city by the Nazis in the Second World War. I visited this site at the end of a cold winter day, just as the sun was setting. The sun was very faint that day, and all that was left was a bit of gray sky. I was quite alone in that vast cemetery save for thousands upon thousands of crows — large black crows making a terrible noise. It was a very dead place. I heard no nightingales; only crows. The so-called realist will look at death and say there are no nightingales' voices, there are only crows; and that, when we talk about life after death or a purpose to death, we are only fantasizing. That is how the artificial realist speaks. But one realist, the creator of all reality, the Divine Sculptor — He made us, and He knows better than we why He made us.

When Michelangelo finished his sculpture of Moses, which is now in the Church of St. Peter in Chains in Rome, he was asked how he was able to produce this powerful figure. "I just took a block of marble, and I chipped away everything that was not Moses," he replied, as Canova would paraphrase centuries later. God does that to us too. If we are faithful to Him, if we make an act of faith that there is a purpose to living and therefore a purpose to what we call dying, He chips away everything that is not us. He knows what is not us. We call it our sins, and He will chip them away if we offer ourselves to Him. That is what is called the "little dying," the daily mortifications, the Acts of Contrition, penance, and above all, Confession.

If people do not go to Confession, it is simply because they do not know that there are chips that need to be knocked away. They think that their soul is just a block of stone. They do not know that there is a marvelous figure waiting to be born. That is why the twentieth century (and continuing into the twenty-first century) was so hard, was so unwilling to avail itself of God's design. It has not realized what God can do if we offer ourselves to Him.

There is one who knows—the one perfect human of the species, the Mother of God. That is why she weeps. She is Our Lady of Joy and Our Lady of Sorrow. And she weeps because she understands what those chips are, and she weeps when her children do not want the sculptor to remove them so that He can form an image according to the design God intended for each of us.

In 1994, John Paul II went to Saragossa and dedicated a shrine that holds some eleven thousand people. That shrine sits right on the spot where, it is believed, from August 29 to September 1, 1953, an image of the Blessed Virgin wept. The pope was convinced that that spot, just like other shrines to our Lady, was worthy of veneration. On November 6, 1994, preaching at the dedication of the shrine, the pope said that Our Lady was weeping for the twentieth century. She was weeping for the tumultuous events—and for all the deaths and suffering—that had taken place in this most catastrophic of centuries.

There were very many crows circling around the twentieth century, as in this present century, and Our Lady weeps because she remembers what happened more than two thousand years ago. She remembers all the crows around the Cross. She has a longer memory than we do. Mothers always have longer memories than their children. And if we do not pray for a happy death, she will pray on behalf of us for our happy deaths, because she knows a happy death is possible. The Church teaches us that prayer is the memory of the Church made alive by the Holy Spirit. If the human memory is left to its own, it is only nostalgia. And it can haunt and depress us and discourage us. But the Holy Spirit breathes through His Church and interprets history and lets us know that it is moving toward a great purpose. So, too, does each one of us have a history, our own biography, moving toward a purpose, and the Sculptor wants to finish what He has begun. He wants to make what seems very old—new! In the Apocalypse, the book of Revelation, it is written:

> Then I saw a new heaven and a new earth; for the first heaven and the first earth had passed away, and the sea was no more. And I saw the holy city, new Jerusalem, coming down out of heaven from God, prepared as a bride adorned for her husband; and I heard a great voice from the throne saying, "Behold, the dwelling of God is with men. He will dwell with them, and they shall be his people, and God himself will be with them; he will wipe away every tear from their eyes, and death shall be no more, neither shall there be mourning nor crying nor pain any more, for the former things have passed away." And he who sat upon the throne said, "Behold, I make all things new." (21:1–5)

He makes our memory new. He makes the past the gate to the future. He makes death the gate to an eternal life. Our Lord says, "No one takes [my life] from me, but I lay it down of my own accord" (John 10:18).

Through the modern age, many lives have been taken away from people by tyrants and demagogues who were persuaded it was their prerogative to do so. Many of us have cooperated by letting them take our lives away. Not so with Our Lord. He resisted the temptation merely to pass away. Satan wanted to take Our Lord's life from Him. He wanted Him to be a materialist. That is why he offered the first Marxist temptation to turn stones into bread. Our Lord said no. So Satan tried to tempt Him with a fascist temptation — the first fascist temptation — to fly, to be a superman. And Our Lord said no.

Then Satan proposed to Our Lord the proposal that He proposes to our nation now, and really to world culture at the end of the twentieth century and into the twenty-first: the temptation to worship him as the king of the world. It is called secularism. And what a tragedy it would be if, having fought so hard — having made so many sacrifices and shed so much blood — to conquer Marxism and fascism, our great nation should succumb to such a dismal lie. For if we worship Satan, He *will* take our lives away. It was through him that death came into the world. Our Lord came into the world to conquer death and transform it into a gateway to His true kingdom. Is it too hard to understand, or do we let our Mother teach us? And she will. For we have the assurance that if we do not pray well enough for a happy death, she will pray on our behalf.

In June 1909, a missionary priest went out to Wyoming to offer Mass in a settlement in Gillette. He traveled by stagecoach on a long trip from a departure site we are unsure of. But he finally arrived at his destination and was received by welcoming Catholics, glad to have a priest and to have Mass, which they had not celebrated in quite a while. They told him that there would be a train passing through that evening around six o'clock and he would have time, if he wished, to see some of the spectacular scenery in the area. They lent him a horse, and he rode out into the trackless wild for an hour or so. Then, to his astonishment, he saw coming over the horizon a kind of white sheet. As he got closer, he realized that there was a young woman waving this sheet, and she led him to a tent. In the tent was her dying brother, about thirty-three years of age. There was a little table upon which she had set a small crucifix, and two candles were already burning. They were waiting for the priest to give Extreme Unction—the Last Rites of the Church. There were no telephones. No message had been given that the priest was coming. This woman had not had contact with that settlement some distance away. The astonished priest asked her how it was that she was waiting for him? And she said very innocently and simply that she and her brother had been taught as children to say three Hail Marys every day for the grace of a happy death. Her brother had been sick, and they prayed. When they realized that day that it was probably the last day of his life, they prayed once more those three Hail Marys, and then she took up her sheet and went outside to wave down a priest.

Our Lady received her Son into her arms when He was taken down from the Cross. And that is a sign to us why she is the Help of Christians, the Mother of the Church, and she really is the Queen of this universe, of angels and of men. This century has been a Marian century, whether or not people have really called upon Our Lady, because she has been calling upon us.

Charles Lindbergh was no Catholic. He was no Christian mystic. He was very much a kind of quixotic pagan. When he was about to fly across the Atlantic, a Catholic woman gave him a medal, a Miraculous Medal, a little medal with the image of Our Lady. He politely took it and thought it would bring him some good luck. So he fastened it on a little hook in the cockpit. He had a hard time staying awake. Many times, toward the end of the flight, he was on the verge of falling asleep completely, which would have meant his death. But that medal kept clinking and keeping him awake. I do not know how he explained how Our Lady did this. He probably had a very simple, so-called scientific explanation.

But the fact is, Our Lady keeps waking us up. She keeps preventing us from falling asleep into that deadly pagan coma of mere nostalgia. She prays for us, so we call upon her to "pray for us now and at the hour of our death."

The Folded Cloth

There have been certain times in history we call "crises," when a decision has to be made. Are the lights going out, or are they coming on? Is the sun setting, or is it rising? That was very literally the question at the beginning of the American adventure.

Benjamin Franklin recalls how, in the deliberations during the Continental Congress, he used to look at the president's chair, a late-eighteenth-century Chippendale, which still resides in Independence Hall. At the beginning of the eighteenth century, Queen Anne chairs were all the fashion. Their namesake was a remarkable woman in many ways—not least of which was her size. So stout was she that, when she died, they needed to bury her in an outsize coffin. The Queen Anne chair, appropriately enough, has heavy legs. The president's more elegant Chippendale had a half sun on the horizon. Franklin said that sometimes during the debate, it seemed to him that the sun was rising, and other times it seemed as if it was setting.

Two thousand years ago, the same question was asked. The sun grew dark over Jerusalem. Did that mean that the world was ending? Or could it possibly be that it was really just beginning? The pagan, the cynic—in fact, almost everybody—would have said it was all over, if not for the world, at least for the Man on the Cross. They saw Him breathing His last, and they had seen a lot of men do that. They were afraid of the sound. That's the old spirit of the old world. When St. Paul writes to the Romans, he says, "You did not receive the spirit of slavery to fall back into fear, but you have received the spirit of sonship. When we cry, 'Abba! Father!'" (8:15). We have a Father in Heaven. The sun is always rising. Wherever it seems to be setting, Our Father is seeing to it that it's being prepared to rise again. We are not orphans in the universe. Things are not ending. No, we are not pagans, subject to fear. However, when a society does become pagan, it lapses back into fear, all kinds of fear—fear of the self, fear of the city, fear of governments, fear of death, fear of life. That is what artificial population control is. If we do not receive that spirit of adoption, we will not call God Our Father. When it seemed that all was ending on the Cross, Our Lord suddenly cried out, "Abba!" He cried out to His Father in His last utterance, "Father, into thy hands I commit my spirit" (Luke 23:46).

The Love between the Son and His Father is the Holy Spirit we receive. That Holy Spirit is God. God is the Father; God is the Son; and God is the Holy Spirit. And this is why it is of the Son's very essence that He calls upon the Father. It is not of our essence. We are not divine. The Holy Spirit is not part of our natural being. The Holy Spirit is endowed to us in Baptism. The Holy Spirit lives in cultures through the Church. We have to be adopted by God, and when we offer ourselves to that adoption, then we, too, can call, "Abba," and we can then realize that the world is not ending, but that all things are being made new—that death leads to life, and that we are not orphans in the universe.

I live in midtown Manhattan, and we have a kind of unholy tradition at Christmastime. We have a crèche outside the church, and inevitably, every Christmas, somebody comes and steals the Holy Child. The last time, they stole the whole Holy Family, so the shrine of the Nativity looked more like the shrine of the flight into Egypt. A lot of things are stolen in my neighborhood. A lot of violence goes on. People are shot; people are killed. The astonishing thing is, you steal one plaster statue of a little baby and the camera crews come in. It is a good Christmas story, of course. But all the local news programs are there, the networks and wire services pick it up, and the news travels around the world.

There is something about the figure of a baby that brings out all our hope and all our fear. All our hope is expressed in the fact of life — new life — and all our fear is symbolized there, too, when the baby is taken away, for there is a fear in every human heart that that is going to happen to us as well. We were all babies. And the world is filled with people who want to take life away.

There is a deep, abiding fear that we will be orphans in the universe. Our Lord cries from the Cross, "Father." A frightened, orphaned world beneath the Cross listens and waits. Our Lord had a guardian father on earth. In his humility, Joseph simply made himself available to the will of God. He chose to accept that will and to offer himself completely as a guardian of the Holy Child and leave it at that. He did not take upon himself any conjugal rights, any other rights, privileges, and pleasures of a Jew of the house of Israel contracting a marriage. He very quietly, very secretly and simply guarded a Child Whose real Father was in heaven. And Joseph trained the human nature of Our Lord, taught Him how to do all the things we teach a baby to do as that baby grows. He taught Jesus how to build things. And we can be certain that Our Lord loved His guardian father. We can be certain that Our Lord wept when Joseph died. Our Lord wept when His friend Lazarus died. Surely, He wept for Joseph. That scene is hardly ever represented — Jesus and Mary burying Joseph.

Of course, Mary knew all about burials. She was a woman who evidently was asked to take charge of community affairs — the wedding at Cana being a prime example. She, like many of the women in the villages of her day, surely practiced some kind of midwifery. This Immaculate Woman, this total presence of humble love, must have been there when sick children in the neighborhood needed some extra attention—when a deformed child was born, when a crippled child needed help walking, and perhaps some family did not have any earthly idea what to do.

I am sure that, many times, Our Lady held the children of mothers who had died in childbirth, and that, many times, she buried little children because many died in her community. Besides being a midwife, Our Lady also helped with end-of-life matters, doing the work of an undertaker. Burying the dead was a woman's role then. If you go to Jerusalem today, you can see the stone, known as the Lithostrotos, where the women anointed Our Lord's body for burial. (The place where the trial before the Crucifixion took place is also called the Lithostrotos.) All of the dead were anointed. And, when Our Lord was taken down from the Cross, Our Lady had some embalming oil—perhaps the myrrh given to her by the "wise man" from a strange, far-away place who came to see her Infant in Bethlehem thirty-three years earlier. Then she wrapped her Son in a shroud. You see a pattern here. Mothers save things, and she probably was saving that cloth ever since she had prepared cloths to wrap around her little baby Boy. Needless to say, He outgrew those little cloths, but one of them was evidently big enough to cover His face when He died. Our Lady and the women who accompanied her helped bury her Son. It was an act of mercy.

In our world today, there are those who are burying Jesus again. Only now, it is an act of cruelty—an act of cruelty against culture, an act of cruelty against themselves. There are those who want to bury Our Lord in our schools, lest anyone hear His Name mentioned. There are those who want to bury Him in all our public entertainments unless His Name is used as blasphemy. There are those who want to bury Our Lord in all our social engagements, in our homes, at our cocktail parties—never mentioning Him seriously. There are those who want to bury Him in our government, in our culture. That is at the heart of the voice that says we have to separate church and state. Well, the state has its rights, and the Church has Her rights, and it is of the divine plan that they should not transgress one another. The Church has been the guardian of that truth, many times, when the government has forgotten it. And when voices in the Church have forgotten it, great saints have been raised up to remind the Church Herself of that truth. But we cannot separate God from government unless the government intends to fall. If the government intends to bury Christ, it ends up burying itself.

You may have heard the line, "The Church shall be separate from the state, and the schools shall be separate from the Church." It appeared in the Constitution of the Soviet Union. No such line appears in the United States Constitution. The architect of that Constitution, James Madison, wrote in June 1785, "Memorial and Remonstrance against Religious Assessments" regarding the First Amendment: "Before any man can be considered as a member of Civil Society, he must be considered as a subject of the Governour of the Universe." How that all works out constitutionally is for the citizenry to understand. But if we try to bury Christ in culture, all we do is lose the cult that gave us culture. It was not all that long ago that Nikita Khrushchev said, "We will bury you." He was looking at us—and there were many of us who believed it. In this is how we got the Cold War, and the fear of the Cold War. But that was the old spirit. That was the old spirit of which St. Paul spoke—the spirit of slavery which engenders fear. If you go to Moscow now, you can visit a convent that has recently reopened, the Convent of the Maidens. Once again, the voices of consecrated women religious are heard singing the daily liturgical offices, and they are praying for the dead who are buried in the cemetery of that convent. And if you go into that cemetery, you will find in one of the graves the bones of Nikita Khrushchev. He has been buried. And that is the story of all of us. That is the story of everyone who has ever been born. We are going to be buried. The question is, are we going to be buried as orphans or as adopted sons and daughters of a Father — a Father in heaven?

A few years back, a well-known journalist who made a career of criticizing the Church and the pope predicted that the pope was going to die very soon, no question about it. He knew enough about medicine, he knew about the actuarial tables, and he knew enough friends in Rome who spread rumors to persuade him that the pope would not outlive the year. At the end of that year, 1994, the pope's picture appeared on the cover of *Time* magazine. Not only had he lived out the year, but he was "Man of the Year" — at the same time visiting the Philippines, where he addressed the largest crowd ever assembled in human history. And, as that event was taking place, the journalist who had assured everyone that the pope would not live out the year, died. In credit to that man, he had requested that, at his funeral, which was held in a Catholic church, the old hymn "Dies Irae" be sung. "O day of wrath, O day of mourning, with David's voice, with cymbal blending, Heaven and earth in ashes ending." It was not a politically correct hymn then or now. We certainly do not hear it very often. There are those who think it has been totally abolished. But it has not been abolished from reality, for there is a day of wrath and there is a day of mourning, and the prophet David's voice, the psalmist's singing, does blend with the pagan cymbal's voice in that common experience of death and the suspicion that death may be the end of everything. And it may very well be that under the panoply of heaven, earth itself will just crumble into ash. It is a song that should be sung, but only in churches. It is incongruous to sing that song outside the Church. When it is sung in church we look up and we see the Cross, and even as it is being sung, we can hear in the background, "Father, Father, Father."

That voice saves our culture from the curse of superficiality — a superficial understanding of babies, of old people, of life and death themselves. St. Bartholomew was skinned alive. If our religion is only skin-deep, we are not going to be very good martyrs if they skin us alive. The voice of God, the fullness of truth, which fulfills all religious longing, must, through the power of the Holy Spirit, penetrate the skin of culture and go to its very heart. And when that happens, we will be able to say, almost as well as Our Lord's own Mother said, "Let it be done to me according to Your word." Surely when she stood with Jesus at the tomb of Joseph, she must have thought that those words were easier said at the beginning than at that moment. But in her immaculate obedience, she kept saying it. "Let it be done."

If we knew everything that has happened to us already in our lives before they happened, would we really have been willing to say, "Let it all happen"? If our nation had known its entire history, would it have been willing to say, "Let all that happen"? Would our culture, looking back upon all the wars and massacres commingled with all our great achievements, have been willing to say, "Let it happen"? Knowing all about Gettysburg and Verdun, going all the way back to Thermopylae and Agincourt and the Crusades and the gulags and the genocides, would we have been willing to say, "Let it happen"? At the end of the twentieth century, would we, knowing what we know now, have been able to say, a hundred years earlier, "Let it all happen"? Would we, looking back on the last twenty years, have been willing to say at the dawn of the twenty-first century, "Let it be done to me according to Your will"?

Our Lady has said it for us. Our Lady simply, day by day, did what was necessary to take care of Joseph and her Son. And because God had prepared her to obey His word, when He came into the world, He was willing in His humility to obey her word. He listened as a child when she said to Him, "It is time to get up," and "It is time to go to bed." He listened to her when she said to Him, "You have to eat your supper." And, being a child, He probably had to be told more than once, "Fold Your clothes. Straighten Your room. Put out the garbage."

Our Lord was taken down from the Cross and placed in the tomb. A few days later, John, being younger, outran Peter to the garden. But he waited outside the tomb for Peter to enter first, for Peter is the chief of the Apostles. And, from that moment on — over the entire course of civilization — the voice of Peter is the first to confirm the brethren in the faith. Peter looks into the tomb, and he sees that the Lord is risen. This is the message that Peter and his successors now proclaim to our culture.

And when Peter looked in, he saw the shroud and also another little cloth — the face cloth — neatly folded and lying separately. Even in eternal glory, Jesus folded His clothes, as His Mother had taught Him.

About the Author

Father George Rutler has long been a pastor of parishes in the heart of New York City. He holds numerous academic degrees from the United States and Europe and is the author of thirty books. He has broadcast programs on EWTN since the early 1980s.